The Job Search Advisor

The Job Search Advisor

Christopher G. Gilliam, SPHR

Writers Club Press
San Jose New York Lincoln Shanghai

The Job Search Advisor

Writers Club Press
an imprint of iUniverse.com, Inc.

For information address:
iUniverse.com, Inc.
5220 S 16th, Ste. 200
Lincoln, NE 68512
www.iuniverse.com

ISBN: 0-595-19601-2

Printed in the United States of America

For my three girls;
Christy, Nakeata, and Syaira
— Christopher

Contents

Acknowledgements

This work would not have been possible without the encouragement, assistance, and patience of my lovely bride. Christy, your belief in me is what keeps me going. Others who played major roles include:

Stephanie Holland	primary edit
Rock Brown	supplemental edit
JoAnn Kachigian	edited 3 chapters
Paul Erway	document recovery project
Jamie Lloyd	cover design
My clients, friends, and family	for sharing their stories and allowing me to make use of their examples

Thank you, to all of you. Your assistance is appreciated more than you can know.

–Christopher G. Gilliam

For the sake of consistency and readability, the author has made use of what is commonly referred to as the "authors prerogative" to modify some of the stories contained herein.

Part I

Preliminaries

Introduction

A minimal job search is what most everybody does when looking for employment. It can take anywhere from just a few minutes to about half a day per week and usually results in frustratingly few interviews and even fewer job offers. This type of job search relies on traditional and typical job search methods-methods that are not very effective. If you are conducting this type of job search, then you need this book.

How do I know? Because I've interviewed you-or at least I've interviewed hundreds like you. In fact, nearly everyone I've ever interviewed has needed at least some of this material, which is why I decided to put it on paper and make it available to you.

There is a better way to conduct a job search than the worn out minimal job search method. This "better way" is what *The Job Search Advisor* is all about. If you are motivated, ambitious, disciplined, and ready to improve your employment outlook, then this book is for you.

Before we actually get into the mechanics of the job search, there are several preliminaries that will need to be covered. Part I speaks to these issues and will prepare you for the second part.

Part II covers just about every aspect of the actual job search. It is the "meat" that I suspect you were looking for when you decided to purchase this book. Using the advice in this part will help you conduct a real job search-one that will result in serious job offers.

Part III is a special bonus section that I hope you will consider thoughtfully-not just for your job search, but for your life!

There are anywhere from several dozen to several hundred published books and articles on each of the areas that are covered in this book. The purpose in writing this book was not to regurgitate all of this previously released and generally known material.

Rather, while I will share some of this basic information, the main thrust will be to share personal insights that I have learned over the years as I've managed the hiring process for private, public, and not-for-profit organizations. You will also find several dozen real-life examples addressing specific issues.

One of the difficulties in writing a book like this is that every job search is different. Rather than write one book for executives, another for mechanics, a third for airline personnel, a fourth for folks seeking to work in the restaurant industry, and so on, I've chosen to put it all in one book.

Therefore, it is imperative that you use common sense as you plan and carry out your job search. What works for some people in a certain industry often won't work for others in the same field, or for other people in different industries. The main principle to remember during your job search is to be yourself.

There is a trite little saying that goes something like this: "Finding a job is a full-time job." Nearly everyone has heard it, and many people say it, but few actually practice it. It is, however, a truthful statement. In my own life, I remember a time this was pointedly brought to my attention when my sister said that she wanted me to find a job so I'd be able to work fewer hours!

Because there is so much that can happen during a job search, this book addresses those of you who have the luxury of being able to devote 40 to 60 hours per week in your pursuit of employment. For those of you who don't have this much time to devote to your search, the information presented here will help you make better use of the time you do have.

Chapter One

Why Are You Conducting a Job Search?

The first thing you need to do is deal with the reason you are conducting a job search. If you are currently happily employed and are simply looking for a better position, then you are in the ideal situation. However, this is not the case for most job seekers.

Consider the following reasons that prompt many job searches:

1. Being laid off
2. Being fired
3. Quitting due to unacceptable circumstances
4. Re-entering the work world after an extended furlough
5. Not being satisfied with a current employment situation

If any of these reasons sound familiar, then you will have emotions that you'll need to deal with during your job search.

There are several stages that nearly everyone goes through when dealing with such things. These stages include denial, shock and panic, anger, sickness (physical or emotional), guilt, rejection, depression and loneliness, self-pity, justification, job-search difficulties related specifically to the reason you are no longer with your last employer, hope, and finally acceptance.

It will be difficult to get far in your job search until you get to the point of acceptance. I'm certainly not saying that you can't conduct a job search until you get to that point, but what I am saying is that until you are there, one of your priorities should be to get to that point.

There are several avenues to help you get there. If you are eligible for any sort of out-placement service or employee assistance program (EAP), you should definitely take full advantage of them. Depending upon your individual situation and financial position, meeting with a professional psychologist or counselor might be a good idea, and many churches also offer excellent counseling services. Another place to try is your local Job Service office because it offers services to help you understand your emotions so you can improve your job search.

There are about as many ways to help you get to the point of acceptance as there are people and situations. For example, sharing your feelings with someone you trust can help get things off your chest and provide you with an objective viewpoint. Making a list of all your positive attributes, things you like about yourself, and successes you've had can help you see yourself in perspective. In addition, time is always a healer. Finally, referring to Part III of this book will most definitely help–if you let it. As you can see, there really are innumerable ways to get yourself back on track. At this point in your job search, it's your job to figure out which will work for you.

The reason that it will be difficult to get very far in your job search until you get to the point of acceptance is that your mental, psychological and emotional health and attitude will influence your entire search. One example is the fact that it's difficult to be excited about actively pursuing the various aspects of a proper job search (covered in Part II) when you're dealing with doubting your own self-worth, or feel that you've been wronged. Another example is that during interviews, if you're still in the stage of bashing your former employer, or justifying why you were innocent of all wrong, the prospective employer with whom you are interviewing will pick up on this and it will work against you.

I once coached an individual who had spent 28 years working for his employer before being laid off. A local newspaper had published an article about the fact that his department was being let go, and he figured that other employers in the area would be familiar with the situation and would therefore be able to understand his negative emotions. He was still in the anger stage and simply couldn't understand that employers wouldn't be interested in hiring a guy who had nothing but bad things to say about his former employer.

So if you are currently, and happily, employed, then I recommend that you charge ahead with your job search. Otherwise, you should pursue your job search while also working on getting to the point of acceptance.

Chapter Two

Self-Evaluation–Career, Personal, and Financial Goals

When you decide it's time to get serious about finding a job, one of the first things you'll need to do is consider what you want out of your professional career. Of course, if you've always truly loved what you do, then you won't have to worry too much about this. However, entirely too many people end up following the path of least resistance and end up spending several years in a profession that they don't particularly enjoy.

One of the best (and sometimes only) times to alter the course of your career is when you are between jobs. Of course, if you are currently employed, you can still gain the knowledge, skills and abilities that you'll need to make a change. You'll just have to make time for this while also working at your full-time job. Whichever is your situation, take some time and reflect on what you're after.

There are dozens of assessments, also called tests, available that can help you do this. A couple of examples include personality assessments, which help people figure out who they are and what they want, and career indicator assessments, which help folks know which type of career might best suit them.

If you don't want to get that elaborate, just spend some time reflecting on what you enjoy doing and on what your ideal job would be. This should be a brainstorming session, so it's imperative that you not limit yourself by what you think might or might not be possible.

For example, let's say you got a job after high school in a factory and you've spent the last 10 years driving a forklift at that same factory. And let's say you've always hated it. If that's the case, why go after another fork-lift-driver job? Let's further say that you love hunting and fishing and talking to new people–things your current job doesn't include. Why not consider a job at an outdoor store, or what about working for the Department of Fish and Game? Neither one of these has much of anything to do with all your experience at the factory. But what about all the time you've spent hunting and fishing on weekends and on vacations? That experience is certainly relevant. And just think, you'd be doing something that you actually enjoy. (What a concept!)

Here's another example. Let's say that after reflecting on what your ideal job might be, you've realized that your ideal job is to be the president of a major corporation. If this is a real possibility for you, then great–go for it. But if you're like the rest of us, the next step is to analyze that ideal job and figure out what it is about that job that you like. Is it the high level of pay? The prestige and respect that such a position commands? The power? Whatever it is about the job that you like, write those things down and then think about what other positions offer those same characteristics. And then pursue one of those jobs.

Of course, before jumping in and pursuing one of these jobs, you would be wise to investigate the career field. You'll want to be fairly certain that it would "fit" you and all the various attributes that are unique to you. These include your interests, financial requirements, personality, and commitment. Your investigation could include the history of the field, as well as how the field is likely to evolve over the next several years. Other items to check out could be key people in the field, relevant technology, competition, trends, etc.

Sharing a real-life example might help at this point. Throughout his 20s, Kyle worked odd jobs and basically lived a carefree life. When Kyle finally decided that it was time to get a "real" job, he did a lot of self-evaluation to find out what he'd been successful at thus far in his life and to find out what he really enjoyed doing. Through this process, he stumbled upon the field of financial management.

Kyle then studied the field to find out what it was, where it had been, where it was going, and whether it would be a good "fit" for him. The self-evaluation and research he conducted helped him make a solid final decision. This decision helped him focus his job search, which subsequently helped him to get that first "real" job. Another benefit of that decision was that he was entering a field that he knew he would enjoy and he could excel.

One thing to keep in mind is that people don't usually start at the top. Therefore, you will want to develop a realistic plan and begin implementation as soon as possible. Furthermore, if you're changing careers you will very likely have to take a cut in pay. Can you do this? Only you can decide that.

Another thing to keep in mind is that you may need to get certain education and experience in order to reach that ideal job. For example, if you really want to be a corporate president, you might very well have to get a master's degree and spend 10 or 20 years in various disciplines (marketing, product management, sales, human resources, purchasing, direct supervision, etc.) in order to get the experience and contacts to be properly groomed for your final destination. But, one thing you can be sure of is it'll never happen if you don't start making it happen.

Remember this: If you continue doing the same things you've always done, then you'll end up staying in the same place that you've always been! I once saw a cartoon that demonstrated this wonderfully. It showed an unshaven, dirty, old bum watching a shiny, smooth limousine drive down the street. Seeing it pass by, the bum said: "There, but for me, goes I."

Chapter Three

Type and Extent of Your Job Search

Most people seem to let their job search just happen to them. They conduct a minimal job search, looking in the classified ads of their local newspaper a few times per week, and maybe letting a couple of friends know that they are looking. This amount of effort can take anywhere from a few minutes to about half a day per week and usually results in a very ineffective job search.

It can also result in a negative cycle that hurts them more and more as time goes on. The reason for this is that after getting very few interviews and job offers they begin to get discouraged, and this shows during any interviews they do get. Because employers shy away from negative people, these people miss out on more and more employment opportunities. The way to prevent this negative cycle in your job search is to determine up front how much time and effort you will devote to your search.

One of the main issues to consider is your financial position. If you absolutely must have income now, then you will not have the luxury of taking your time during your job search. This, of course, will result in your not being able to be as choosy in your employment options. You may have to go out and get a "job"–and then do what you can to get a "career" position.

At this point, allow me to make just a quick little note on going out and getting a "job" job. What I'll be mentioning here is not what this book is about, but I know that some people need to hear it, so here goes. I firmly believe that anybody can go out any day of any week and get a "job" job. Minimum wage, manual labor, flipping burgers, waiting tables, washing dishes, sweeping or shoveling parking lots–the list goes on indefinitely. You might have to cut your hair, shave, take a bath, wash your clothes, and act respectfully, and you might have to inquire at many businesses, but somebody will hire you for something. I know you can do it because anybody can and because people always find jobs when they truly dedicate themselves to the effort. One of my favorite examples is when a client told me about a time during the summer after her seventh-grade year when she was only 12 years old. She got a job cleaning cages at a local pet store!

Another example happened to a client back in '93. He had heard that it took the average white-collar professional nine months to find employment. (Luckily that figure is nowhere near accurate in today's job market.) He had moved to a new city and knew that he could not survive nine months without income. Therefore, he got a job as a waiter at a restaurant to provide some income (not to mention discounts on food) while he continued his job search. He did not enjoy waiting tables, but that didn't matter. He knew it was temporary, and it was ideal because he usually worked nights, which left his days free to do his regular job search activities.

So if you need to go out and get a "job" job to relieve some financial pressures, then go do it. Otherwise, if your savings, unemployment benefits, spouse's income or any other means of support is enough to sustain you for a while, then you may have the luxury of being able to take your time.

The question, then, is how should you use that time? Realizing that it could take some time to secure the right job, you might (wisely) choose to dive right in and commit your full attention to the job of finding a job. However, depending upon your own personal and individual situation, you might decide to enjoy not having to go to work every day.

One person I counseled, for example, had just lost her job. Based on my advice, she analyzed her personal situation and decided that she had about six months to find another job. She then decided to take the first half of that time and only do a minimal job search. This allowed her to pursue some interests that she'd wanted to pursue but had never had the time for. After about three months had passed, she kicked up her job search efforts and devoted much more time to it.

The important thing to realize here is that the affected individual made two decisions. First, she analyzed her situation and figured out how much time she had. Second, she decided how she'd use that time. By "wasting" the first half of the time she had available to her, she fully realized the risk she was taking, but she chose to accept that risk—namely, that it might be difficult to find suitable employment in only three months. Furthermore, she didn't fall into that negative cycle mentioned previously because she knew not to expect too much from her minimal job search.

Her job search didn't just "happen" to her. She made it happen by the choices she made up-front. She evaluated the risks and chose to do only a minimal job search at first, followed by a more in-depth one a bit later. Having made these decisions, it was much easier for her to have a positive attitude about not getting a job right away. After all, she knew that she couldn't expect many interviews and job offers during the first three months because she hadn't really been applying herself. And, after she made these decisions and communicated them to her family and friends, her loved ones were better able to understand why she wasn't out there hitting the streets every day to get a job.

All of the above is great if you are out of work. If, however, you are currently working, stay there till you secure another job. It's almost always easier to find a job when you have a job. It's sort of a subconscious thing to employers. They think that if you were really a valuable employee you'd be working for somebody somewhere.

The final thing to consider when determining the extent and type of job search you will conduct is where are you looking? In other words, are you conducting a national, regional, or local search? Obviously, the smaller the area you choose, the less opportunity you give yourself to find a job. However, if you can't move for whatever reason, you'd definitely be wasting your time to consider employers in other areas. Throughout your job search, you must remember that you are working for yourself. Your job is to find a job. Spend your time wisely.

Chapter Four

Most Qualified vs. Best Match

Employers rarely look for the most qualified person for a job. What they want is the best match. For example, a person with 30 years of relevant experience and a doctorate degree in the field might appear to be the most qualified applicant. However, he or she probably isn't the best match if the position only pays minimum wage.

In the above example, most people would think of the applicant as being "overqualified." Hiring managers who understand employment law typically don't like this word because a person is either qualified or not qualified, and beyond that it's a matter of "fit." Realizing that it really is just a matter of semantics, even those of us who don't like the word "overqualified" find ourselves using it. The reason for this is that nearly everyone understands that word, and they usually have difficulty grasping the "best match" concept.

You must keep this in mind when talking with employers. They want the best match in hopes that the person selected will be a positive contributor and stay with the company for years to come. You should want the best match too, so that you'll be happy at your new place of employment and feel sufficiently challenged, appreciated, and respected.

If employers were only looking at your qualifications, they wouldn't need to meet with you. All they'd have to do would be to review applications and resumes and make a hiring decision based on the information provided.

In the previous example, minimum wage was the reason that the applicant with the doctorate wasn't the best match. That was an extreme example, but the principle works the same no matter what numbers you're using. For example, if the position was approved at a pay grade that pays $50,000 to $60,000 a year, and the most you've ever made was $35,000, then the employer probably won't think you have the necessary experience to handle the level of responsibilities that he needs you to handle.

Conversely, if you are used to being paid $80,000 a year, then employers are likely to reject you because they fear you won't be sufficiently challenged, or that you'll leave as soon as you can find another job paying what you had been making previously.

Assuming that you meet the minimum qualifications for the position, your salary history is certainly not the only other thing employers seek when looking for the right fit. It is, however, about the most objective, black-and-white thing they can look at.

Another big consideration that employers look for is how your personality will fit with the specific team they already have established. If they currently have a smooth-running machine, they won't want to introduce a new person who doesn't fit in with the rest of the team.

Aside from looking for a fit with the specific people that you would be working for and with, employers also look for an overall fit with the company. If you are a tennis shoes, jeans, and T-shirt sort of person and the place you're applying at insists upon three-piece suits and cowboy boots, then the employer will likely figure that you might try to buck the system.

Other "fit" items can include your professional career goals, your interpersonal skills, and your ability to multi-task, remain focused, meet deadlines, and communicate. Your ambition, creativity, energy level, and well-roundedness can also play into the decision. As you can imagine, there are many traits employers look for when hiring. This is one reason it is so important to look and act your best during your job search. It is also an awful good reason to do as much research as you can on an employer before you interview, so you have an idea of what the employer is looking for!

In conclusion, here are a couple of real-life scenarios. First of all, when an employer says you are overqualified for a position, remember that what he or she probably means is that you were not the best match. Rather than argue, which will get you nowhere, just accept the fact that everybody is not a perfect fit for every position. Furthermore, just because you didn't get the offer doesn't mean the employer didn't think you could have done the job, or even that you weren't a good match. The employer just didn't think you were the best match!

Finally, I can't begin to tell you the number of times that people I've interviewed have called me up to say that they should have gotten the job because they know they are more qualified than the person who was hired. This is not a good tactic if you ever want to get hired by that employer. If you are the type of person who might make such a call, then please listen one more time to the theme of this chapter: Employers don't just look for people who are qualified to do the work, they look for "fit" and ultimately for the "best match."

Chapter Five

Attitude and Honesty

Employers hire who they like. Your attitude will determine, to a large extent, how much they like you. One study showed that an employer considers three things when hiring. While these skills are the key to get you in the door, they only account for 10 percent of what is considered. Appearance accounts for another 10 percent, and attitude accounts for 80 percent!

It's very difficult to like somebody who is negative and doesn't openly share information. If this describes you, then you might need to work on adopting a more positive communicative attitude. Getting the job you want may depend upon it!

If you're involved in an extensive job search that's taking several months or even years, or if your personal or financial life is falling in ruins around you, it's very easy to develop a bad attitude. Don't let this happen to you! Besides the information shared in Chapter 1 on this subject, one of the best ways to maintain a positive attitude is to stay busy. Busy, that is, looking for a job.

Since it's your job to find a job, you should treat it as such. For example, you should have a regular schedule, one that includes being showered, dressed appropriately, and "on the job" by 8:00 in the morning. You should also have a list of things to do every day. This list could include quotas for such things as a certain number of networking calls, hours of employer research, or numbers of interviews. For more on what you should be doing, refer to Part II of this book. Following the advice in that part would take at least 40 to 50 hours per week.

Honesty is another characteristic you must have. This will be stated throughout this book, but it is mentioned here as part of the "preliminaries" because of how very important it is. You must be honest. On your resume, in your interviews, and everywhere else, you must tell the truth.

This is especially noteworthy based on the statistics that show most people misrepresent themselves on their resumes and during interviews. Because hiring professionals know this, we are on the lookout for anything suspicious. Naturally, if we suspect something fishy, we check it out if we can. If we can't check it out, we will oftentimes go with our "gut feel," and you end up being weeded out of the selection process.

And, even if you make it through that process and get hired, most employers will release you if they discover at a later date that you misrepresented yourself. The chances of getting caught are just too high, and so is the price you have to pay if and when you are caught.

This does not mean that you have to explain all the sordid details about every bad thing that's ever happened to you. But, if a question is raised, handle it with integrity. The key is to accept responsibility for your actions. It might also help if you are able to show documentation or tell specific examples that can substantiate whatever you claim as being part what you have to offer.

Chapter Six

What Is "H.R." and Why Do We Need It?

After retiring from a successful career with one employer, my dad began looking for work in another industry. There's one comment that I've always remembered him making while he was conducting his job search. In anger and frustration he said that for the life of him he couldn't understand why he had to interview with young people who knew nothing about the type of work he did. Many years later, I became one of those people.

It can be very frustrating for good, hard-working people to have to be interviewed by an H.R. (Human Resource) person. This is especially true if they don't understand H.R.'s role in the process or the process itself.

Most large employers have a Human Resource Department that job candidates must deal with to get hired. Dealing with H.R. personnel can be a frustrating experience. They can seem to be a bottleneck and seriously slow down the hiring process. But, if you understand the reason for their involvement, it can definitely help your attitude when dealing with them.

I'll introduce this reason by sharing the response I gave to one client who was thinking of getting into the field of H.R. He said that he thought he'd like it, except for the fact that a lot of what H.R. people do seems to be a game. I agreed that it was a game. But when you're in H.R., it's your game!

The point is that H.R. is involved because recruitment is H.R.'s responsibility. And it has to be. Employers have three main reasons for needing H.R. people to handle the recruitment efforts.

First, there are so many laws and court cases regulating the hiring process that companies can hardly afford not to have such a department. Part of H.R.'s job is to make sure that the employer is consistent in how it deals with applicants. So H.R. personnel write policies and procedures in an effort to achieve this consistency. This consistency then helps employers prove that they weren't practicing discrimination during their recruitment efforts.

For example, a manager might decide that she wants to hire a certain applicant and might even tell the applicant that he has the job. However, if all the proper paperwork isn't filled out, H.R. might have to step in and insist that it gets completed before a formal job offer is made. This frustrates everyone involved: the manager who needs the person, the applicant who was told that he had the job, the other candidates who are applying for the job because they must wait longer for a decision, and the H.R. personnel. H.R. personnel often are accused of slowing down the hiring process when they are really just doing their jobs by protecting the employer.

Let me share an example of why consistency is so important. Let's say the person the manager wanted to hire was a white male under 40 years of age. If the company moved ahead with the hire without going through the regular procedures, then next time an older job candidate, or a minority candidate, applied, the company could find itself in court. These candidates could file complaints saying they were discriminated against because they were required to complete many procedures although past job candidates were able to skip these formal processes.

Because the company treated its applicants inconsistently, it could end up spending many years and hundreds of thousands of dollars in legal costs trying to defend itself.

The second reason employers need H.R. people to handle their hiring is because recruitment campaigns require a lot of time and effort. Developing and implementing a recruitment strategy, screening applicants, handling position inquiry calls, making sure necessary paperwork is completed, and arranging interview schedules are just a few of the time-consuming activities involved. Quite frankly, supervisors and managers have more important things to do than worry about hiring.

This is why when applying for a job you can't expect to work only with the particular manager who has the opening. Managers are too busy to deal with all the details of the hire, which is why they generally refer you to H.R.

And what about the argument that the H.R. representative doesn't know the job? The answer to this question is the third reason employers need H.R. departments. More than likely, if you're invited for an interview the employer has already decided that you meet the minimum qualifications for the job. The employer determines this after reviewing items such as your resume and application, and doing a phone interview. In other words, the employer knows you can do the job.

When you're invited in for an interview, the employer will want to verify the information on your application and see if you'll fit in with the rest of the company. They want to check out such things as your interpersonal, organizational, and communication skills, work ethic, integrity, ability to focus, and overall attitude. Intrinsic skills like these are what the H.R. representative is specifically looking for.

Remembering this will help you understand the section on dealing with H.R. in Chapter 17, where you'll learn that you don't need to share too many technical details with the H.R. person. You'll want to save that stuff for a hiring manager who will actually understand it!

In my professional recruiting experience, I have interviewed high-level executives, doctors, engineers, airline pilots, CPAs, architects, computer professionals, and many other highly educated and technical people. How could anyone expect me to know everything about each of these fields? And yet in all these situations, I was able to screen out several folks who were not a good fit with the particular employer for whom I was working. By doing this, I saved the hiring managers dozens of hours of wasted time.

Today's business world is both litigious and team oriented. Because of these two dynamics, few employers allow a hiring decision to be made by just one person. Depending upon the organization, the "fit" decision that the H.R. representative makes is sometimes weighed just as heavily as, or even more than, a person's technical skills.

Remember the chapter called "Most Qualified vs. Best Match"? Sometimes a hiring manager's decision-making ability is biased toward a certain applicant because of the applicant's abundant qualifications or because the manager desperately needs to hire someone as soon as possible. Such a bias might cause the hiring manager to overlook personality traits that wouldn't fit well in the organization. In such a situation, the H.R. representative is able to offer an objectivity that could save the organization headaches in the future.

During your job search, you must not become frustrated with H.R. representatives. Doing so will only cut your chances of being hired because, remember, it's their game. Usually, the H.R. representative is the one person you must please before you're permitted to see anyone else in the company. I'd recommend that you go into each H.R. interview thinking "H.R. is my friend." How's that for a sales pitch on Human Resources?

Part II

The Job Search

Chapter Seven

Where Are the Jobs?

Networking is the best place to learn of job openings. It is basically making friends for the purpose of improving your employment opportunities. If it doesn't come naturally to you, or if you're not a "people person," then this is an area you should research. To learn more on networking, review Chapter 13.

The Internet has become extremely popular with both employers and job seekers. If you don't have a computer with Internet access at home, check for one at the local public library, schools in your area (elementary, secondary, as well as colleges and universities), Job Service and other state agencies, folks in your "network" (friends, family, and your church), and employment counseling services. And finally, some businesses exist solely to make money by renting time on their computers. Look for those in the Yellow Pages.

Professional recruiters and temporary agencies are other sources for jobs. Each of these has pros and cons, so you need to be cautious when dealing with these businesses. Read about these services in Chapter 25 to become more knowledgeable on what they offer and what some of their downsides are.

Many employers, especially the larger ones, have employment hotlines. This is typically a toll-free call if the employer is outside your area. When you call these hotlines, you are generally greeted with a recording that takes you through the company's current openings and then lets you know how to apply. The jobs often change frequently, so you should call every week or two.

Visiting employers is another way to discover job openings. Quite often, companies post openings in their Human Resource departments. Even when a posting is for current employees only, it wouldn't be too early for you to begin the application process, as long as you go about it carefully and don't come across as someone who doesn't follow directions. If you make a habit of visiting companies regularly to review job openings, you might end up making a contact or two with the receptionist, secretary, or an H.R. representative, which could help you in the future.

Career fairs are also good places to meet prospective employers. Some companies do nothing but host career fairs, and newspapers and radio stations sponsor them, too. Employers also sponsor career fairs, either on site, at the local Job Service office, or at some other location. As you review your local newspaper, be sure to be on the lookout for these and attend if at all possible.

Colleges and universities also sponsor career fairs, and while these are specifically for their students, you might be able to wander in and make some connections that you wouldn't have been able to otherwise.

If you are a college graduate, you can probably take advantage of your school's employment placement office. If you are not a college graduate, or if your school is too far away or doesn't offer such assistance, you might call the placement office of a nearby school to see if you could use its services anyway. Who knows, you might get lucky.

Taking advantage of any services available through tax-funded agencies is also worthwhile. I've mentioned Job Service several times throughout this book, and while I wouldn't spend an exorbitant amount of time there, it's certainly worth finding out what services it offers. Remember, you should pursue all options.

Another tax-funded agency to check is the state Personnel Commission. (It might go by a different name in your state.) A lot of state jobs are never advertised, and even though you'd be able to find out about them at your local Job Service, this branch of your state government might be able to offer assistance, too.

If you're open to working for the federal government, you should contact the United States Office of Personnel Management (OPM). If the military is something you would consider, you could contact a recruiter from the branch you're be interested in. (Did you know that you can usually join the Army National Guard until age 35?)

Other public sector opportunities are available through your city and county/borough/ parish personnel offices. So if you're open to public sector employment, there are many avenues to pursue.

One avenue I've heard about is a little morbid, but it makes sense. Review the obituaries. When people die, if they had jobs, it's fairly likely that their employers will need to replace them.

A similar tactic, though nowhere near as morbid, is to review the engagement, wedding and birth announcements in the newspaper. Oftentimes, when people get married, one or the other must move. Other times, when a new child is introduced to the family, one parent decides to stay home. Either way, the employer must look for a replacement.

Yet a third tactic along the same lines is to review the section of the paper that mentions promotions and advancements. When people are promoted, they often leave an opening behind them that must be back-filled. And, of course, any significant changes with the employer itself can create openings, such as relocations, expansions, taking on new product lines, etc. When such things happen, you certainly shouldn't wait until the employer takes out an ad to begin applying for a position.

A different approach you could try (if you are really willing to try anything) is to take out an ad yourself. While this might not be viewed as overly professional, depending upon the type of work you are looking for (and where you are conducting your job search), it might be appropriate. There's certainly no law that says that employers are the only side of the desk that can advertise. It definitely would show employers that you are available and ambitious.

Regular advertisements are, of course, another place to look. Employers place ads in newspapers, trade journals and trade magazines. For simplicity's sake, we will begin our discussion with newspaper ads, and then go on to journals and magazines. However, please realize that most of what will be presented is sound advice no matter what the type of publication.

Newspaper ads are still used fairly frequently and should be a regular part of any job search. You should pay special attention to the Sunday edition. The best daily paper to check is usually the Monday edition, and Wednesday generally follows as the next best.

It wouldn't hurt to contact the newspaper directly and ask if it has a special "career opportunity" section. Sometimes a newspaper will have such a section one day a week and offer employers substantial price reductions for advertising in it.

Moving on, let's look at where in the newspaper you should, or could, look. Basically, you should look in different sections. Some newspapers list all positions alphabetically. In these cases, you'll want to look under the many various titles that a position you'd want could be under. For example, a computer wizard would look under "C" for computers, "I" for information technology, "S" for systems, "P" for programmers, etc.

Other newspapers list positions by category, such as Engineering, Technical, Computer Technology, Health Related, Management/Professional, etc. Even with these papers, you'll want to scan the various sections because some positions can easily fall under more than one heading.

Another thing to be aware of is that display ads are often not in the area you'd think they should be in due to their size. Display ads are the fancier ones that are normally in a square or rectangular box and are usually at least two columns wide. Therefore, be sure to scan all the display want ads, just in case.

Yet another thing to know is that if an employer has several positions to advertise, it is likely to put them all together into one ad. In doing so, positions with little to no similarities might be right next to each other. In these cases, it's impossible to be in the "correct section" of the paper for all the positions. So the employer must decide in which section to put the ad.

If a majority of the positions are technical, then that might be the section it goes in, even though there might be a non-technical position, too. Or, if it's a health-related business, that might be the section it goes in, even though there might be non-health-related positions listed. So, you should scan all the large ads in all the various sections of the publication to be sure you don't miss the one position that you are looking for.

If you have decided to expand your job search (regionally, nationally, or even worldwide), don't feel that you actually have to subscribe to all of the various publications. A simple trip to your local library should provide you with all the out-of-area papers that you'll need.

Trade magazines and journals related to your particular profession are another method employers use to find the people they are looking for. While some trade magazines do have employment sections, employers may decide not to list positions there. For example, one employer once told me that she liked to place employment ads elsewhere in the magazine. The thought behind this is that only people actually looking for work bother to look at the employment section.

Sometimes, employers would rather target folks who are already employed, so advertising in the regular section of the magazine, alongside articles, might attract these particular people. Realizing this, you should flip through the entire magazine, which you should do anyway as part of your research.

When you first begin your job search, it's a good idea to review the major newspapers within your search area, as well as any trade journals and magazines, for the last eight to 12 weeks. It is not unusual for employment searches to drag on for months, and there's no reason for you to let all the employment opportunities from the last few months pass you by. Besides, this will give your job search a kick-start, which it might need at the beginning.

Aside from newspapers within your search area, and trade magazines related to your field, there are a couple of other types of publications that you should check out. One is the various magazines and newspapers produced for college students. The goal of most college students is to get a job one day, and realizing this, many employers advertise to catch students' attention. I suggest you visit your local college or university and review some of these publications. You might just find a lead that will result in your next job!

Another type of publication specifically targets job seekers. These only list positions available. These publications sometimes don't even have any articles or feature stories; they are nothing but want ads. There are several dozen of these. National Business Employment Weekly, Federal Jobs Digest, and International Employment Gazette are three of them, just to name a few. Career fair companies publish others. As you conduct your job search you'll undoubtedly run across some of these, and when you do, be sure to review them.

Chapter Eight

First Impressions and Appearance

They say that you only have one opportunity to make a first impression. This is both true and false. When you first meet an interviewer, he will form a first impression. However, he also had a first impression the first time he reviewed your resume, another when he spoke to your answering machine or voice mail in an attempt to contact you, and yet another when he finally got to speak with you to set up the interview.

And what about the first impression he got when his associate (who happens to be in your "network") recommended you, or when he saw you from a distance at the last professional luncheon? Another first impression can be formed when the receptionist tells him about your attitude and conduct when you came in (or even called in) for an application.

Throughout your job search, employers' first impressions (no matter how many of them there may be) should be of primary importance to you. Your application, resume, cover letter, and phone calls are all ways you make first impressions. This is why everything you provide to a potential employer must be neat, legible, and spelled correctly, must make proper use of grammar and punctuation, and must be focused and concise.

This is also the reason you must use a good phone voice and practice proper phone etiquette. Anytime you are on the phone (whether you're talking to someone or simply recording a message onto the answering machine or voice mail) be sure to smile while you're doing it. I mean this literally. Actually smile when you talk. It may sound strange to you, but it's a fact that people can "hear" whether you are smiling. And because employers prefer to hire positive people, you need this subtle message communicated.

This is no less important if you decide to have your spouse, child, neighbor, or friend answer the phone or record a message for you. No matter whose voice it is, it needs to communicate that you are a professional, positive person. Employers want to hire people who are emotionally healthy and this is just one of many ways that you can communicate you are such a person.

The message on your answering machine or voice mail should be focused and fairly no-nonsense. Here's an example. "Hello, and thank you for calling. We're not in right now, so if you'd please leave your name, phone number, and the best time to return your call, we'll try to do so at that time. Thanks again, and please wait for the tone."

This does not mean, however, that you can't use the answering machine to give employers subtle messages. These messages could include that you are married (employers generally equate this with stability), have family values ("We're all down at the county fair, so please call back."), or are physically fit ("I'm not currently in because my intramural softball team is playing for the championship today."). Incidentally, a sports-related message also communicates that you are a team player and a winner.

Now let's talk about your physical appearance. While you're out there networking and interviewing you need to be absolutely certain that you look your absolute best.

As far as what you should wear, the simple rule is that you should dress for the particular job for which you are applying. A general rule of thumb for any white-collar job is a suit and tie for men, and a suit or skirt and jacket for women. Generally, you can't go wrong if you dress this way. However, some employers actively promote a casual dress code. In such cases, you might consider dressing as they dress. (When in Rome, do as the Romans do.)

The importance of a good suit can't be overstated. When one young client was first looking for white-collar employment, he wore dress slacks and a sports jacket to interviews. He thought it looked fairly professional; however, I recommended that he invest in a good suit or he would end up with a second-rate job.

I told him about a retail store that specialized in used suits from wealthy executives. This was not your typical second-hand store. It was a place where business people would take their dress clothes after they'd only worn them once or twice, if at all. Nearly everything in the store was in style.

Before making a purchase, he went to several men's stores and got to know the name brands of the best suit makers in the world. He then went to the store I recommended and found a name-brand suit that normally sells for $600 to $1,000, and he only had to pay $50! It fit pretty good, but he knew that "pretty good" wasn't good enough. After all, he wasn't looking for a "pretty good" job. After having it tailored, which cost another $50, he had an excellent top-of-the-line suit for just over $100!

He then spent another hundred or so on name-brand dress shoes, followed by a new dress shirt, a fashionable tie, and other such items. By the time he finished, he had spent only $250, yet he looked like a million!

If you want a really good job, you have to dress for it. And, as you can see from the above example, getting the proper clothes doesn't have to cost you a lot.

Once you have the clothes, you'll want to have the suit dry-cleaned and the shirts laundered with starch and then ironed. For men, if you don't know how to tie a proper knot in a tie, you might need to get a book from the library and practice until you've got it.

Your dress shoes should definitely be shined. If you have the advantage of having been in the military, you can undoubtedly handle this yourself. Otherwise, you might need to get creative. One client, for example, lived about 20 miles outside of a major city. Wanting to look his absolute best, before any interview he would make that 40-mile round trip drive so he could go to the ritziest hotel to have the shoeshine guy do the job. It was the hotel frequented by the U.S. president and movie stars when they are in that city. He figured that the shoeshine guy there had to be the best, and he wasn't going to settle for anything less!

If you're applying for more of a blue-collar job, then you may wear a suit, but this could do you more harm than good. For such positions, it's generally best to dress in clean clothes that are in good shape and fit properly. It is usually a good idea not to try to out-dress the interviewer. He or she might not appreciate this and may end up thinking that you wouldn't fit into the environment.

Here are some specifics:

- Choose a button-down shirt over a T-shirt.
- Don't wear T-shirts, hats or other clothing with slogans that advertise your personal views.
- Make sure your clothes fit properly. If they're too loose or too tight, you'll make a negative impression on the interviewer.
- Make sure your clothes are clean and free of holes and tears.
- Make sure your clothes are in style and not from a decade or two ago.
- Don't wear shorts, unless the job specifically allows it (when applying for a position as a lifeguard, for example).
- Men should wear a clean, white T-shirt underneath the button-down shirt.

When you are conducting a job search, you should pay even more attention to grooming than you did before your very first date. First, make sure to have a good night's sleep the night before an interview or networking opportunity. Next, be sure to give yourself several hours to get ready. This way, you won't get yourself frustrated and filled with anxiety. A recent and decent haircut is important, and you should do this three to five days before your interview. Otherwise, it will look too "new." A thorough shower, making sure to scrub the entire body and every single hair on your head is also a must.

Long hair and earrings on guys? Pierced noses, tongues or other body parts? Amount of makeup to be worn? Gaudy or too much jewelry? These are touchy subjects for a lot of people. Basically what you must keep in mind is that you'll want to look like you'll fit into whatever environment you want to join. All of these things can have a drastic effect on whether you get the job. Please remember, being hired is not based upon your qualifications alone. This may not seem fair, but it's the real world, and depending upon how badly you want or need a job, you'll need to act, dress, and groom accordingly!

Let's now move on to posture, body language, and facial expressions. You can dress sharply, use your most professional and courteous tone of voice, and be groomed better than anyone, but if you're not in command of these aspects, they can ruin an employer's entire impression of you.

Be sure to carry yourself erect and don't slouch. Stand, walk, and sit straight, with your shoulders back. Maintain eye contact without staring the other person down. Be sure to extend a dry, firm hand anytime a handshake is appropriate. If your handshake is not strong, practice with a friend who does have such a handshake. Firm handshakes are appropriate when shaking with women too, and they appreciate it as much as men.

If you are being escorted anywhere, be sure to keep up with the person escorting you if you are physically able. Employers maintain an extremely fast pace. Such a pace is expected of all the employees. It always amazed me when I'd lead able-bodied people somewhere during an interview and they'd end up trailing 20 feet behind because they couldn't keep up. I'd fig-ure that if they couldn't keep up when they were supposedly showing me the best they had to offer, then they'd never keep up with the pace if they actually got the job. So guess what? They'd end up not getting the job. Don't let this happen to you.

During the interview, it's generally a good idea to sit forward in the chair. Be sure to keep your eyes open and maintain a facial expression that communicates that you are interested in what is being discussed. Don't cross your arms, and be sure to have a pleasant look on your face. A smile is a good idea, but if this is difficult for you, then at least practice a pleasant look in front of a mirror.

There are entire books on body language, grooming, dressing for success, and other such matters. If this is not an area in which you are particularly knowledgeable, then you need to spend some of your research time learning all you can about these subjects.

One last thing. Immediately before any interview, or any other situation where you might get to meet a prospective employer, always laugh heartily for a good 10 to 15 minutes. Seriously! Pull your car over or take a walk around the block and make yourself break out in laughter. This is somewhat difficult to do for the first few minutes, but then as you realize how silly you look, it'll begin to be real laughter.

The reason for doing this is so that you'll walk into the interview with a real smile on your face and a twinkle in your eye. It'll help make you look healthy and alive. And if you forget to maintain the smile throughout the interview, at least your facial muscles will still be coming down from a "happy look."

Chapter Nine

Responding to Advertisements

Advertisement costs are fairly high. A simple newspaper display ad, for example, costs several thousand dollars in most major metropolitan areas. Magazine ads cost several thousand dollars, too. Employers are extremely sensitive to these expenditures.

The larger the ad, the more it costs. And to make matters worse, a lot of ad space must be used for the company name, logo, address, description, and application instructions. Depending upon an employer's budget, and its willingness to invest in its recruitment program, there may not be much space left for position descriptions and qualification requirements.

Because of this, these ads only include the most important responsibilities and qualifications of each position. You can bet that employers don't waste space with trivial or secondary responsibilities. Furthermore, attempting to get the most for their money, they exercise extreme economy with how they say what they say. Therefore, if you are responding to an advertisement, you should pay extremely close attention to what it says and how it says it.

For example, if you have 10 years of related experience, and two years of actual experience using the specific skills mentioned in the ad, emphasize those two years more than the 10, even if they were quite a while ago. This does not mean, however, that you completely throw out all the other experience. Just reduce the amount of time (in an interview) and space (on a resume) devoted to the 10 years of related experience so you can give more attention to the two years of specific experience.

Naturally, you may need to adjust your emphasis as you learn more about the position through the interview process, your research, your networking, or any other means by which you discover that the employer would be interested in your other areas of expertise.

Using the previous example, your cover letter and resume would have spoken specifically to the items mentioned in the ad. However, during the interview, you might discover that the employer hopes to grow the position into one that handles other responsibilities, such as those you had in your last 10 years. In this case, you should begin to elaborate on those 10 years. Please note, however, that you should not elaborate until you learn the interviewer is interested.

Unless the focus of the position changes, as it did in the above example, you should stick to the rule of remaining focused on what the ad had asked for. This is especially important if you are switching fields. An interviewer might be intrigued by your unrelated experience and ask more questions than she should. This could allow the interview to trot along nicely, but when you leave, the interviewer is likely to put you in the "no" pile based on her perception that you don't meet the qualifications.

You can keep this from happening to you by consistently answering interview questions with terminology and phrases from the ad. If there isn't an obvious link from the question the interviewer has asked to the position for which you are applying, make use of the transferable skills that are pertinent.

The main reason to use the exact terminology the ad used is because your resume might have to pass through an initial screener, such as an H.R. representative, before it'll ever get to a hiring manager. H.R. personnel typically don't know your field and its terminology as well as you and the hiring manager do, and very often they only look for the specific key words used in the ad.

When hiring for an attorney, for example, the hiring manager might have told the initial screener to look for "co-ownership" experience. He may have used this simple language so the initial screener would better understand what he was talking about. On your resume, however, you might mention your experience with "tenancy in common." While you and the hiring manager might know that these are about the same thing, the screener probably wouldn't know this. And since the screener didn't see the specific words he was told to look for, your resume would be put in the "no" pile.

The same type of thing can happen with acronyms and other abbreviations. For example, if a hiring manager asked the screener to look for someone with experience with the Americans with Disabilities Act or Visual Basic, the screener might not automatically know to look for any mention of "ADA" or "VB" experience, too.

Furthermore, as our society becomes more automated, some companies (especially larger ones) are scanning resumes into a computer and letting the computer do the screening. The computer might only search for the exact words used in the ad, so make sure to use the same terminology in your cover letter and resume.

After the initial screen, you could loosen up and use other phrases (like "tenancy in common" instead of "co-ownership") as you talk to other people in the hiring process who understand the terminology.

Another reason to review an ad carefully is to see if it contains any hidden meanings. You can sometimes pick up a lot of information about a position this way. For example, if the ad asks candidates to have exceptional team leadership skills, could the company be hinting that the current team has problems you'd be expected to fix?

Here are a few more examples. A position titled "administrative assistant" might just be a big title for a receptionist. Examining the ad closely would help you determine your interest in such a position. Asking for someone with excellent communication skills could be indicative of a work environment that is in desperate need of better communication.

Asking for the ability to multi-task could indicate the company has fairly unrealistic expectations, such as expecting the successful candidate to do the work of two or three people. If the ad indicates the salary range, this could give you a good clue as to the expectations, too.

Just as you wouldn't highlight the negative aspects of your employment history, a company won't highlight the negative aspects of its work environment. So, it's up to you to discover the possible downside of each position for which you interview.

Not all ads have hidden meanings. Reading each ad carefully can help you determine questions to ask folks in your network, do some extra research on, or ask about during an interview.

Chapter Ten

Cover Letters

A cover letter is used when submitting a resume. A letter of application is used when inquiring about a job or submitting an application. The purpose of these letters is to introduce yourself, to tell how you can benefit the employer, to persuade the employer to read your resume or application, and to request an interview. For the purposes of this chapter we will discuss cover letters; however, most of the information is relevant to letters of application also.

A cover letter should be sent with every resume whenever you are conducting a serious job search. Of course, if you've decided that you are only conducting a minimal job search, then you don't need to bother with cover letters.

A cover letter gives you the chance to set yourself apart from all the other employment candidates. Your cover letter should include your name, address, and phone number. Be sure to include your area code if you're applying for positions out of your area.

Your address and phone number should be on every single sheet of information that you send to the employer. Why? Because mistakes shouldn't happen, but they do. One time an employer I knew interviewed several candidates for a particular position and somehow lost the resume of the candidate of choice. Luckily the employer had his cover letter. However, his cover letter didn't have his address or phone number.

The candidate ended up not getting the job offer because the employer couldn't get in touch with him.

A cover letter should always be addressed to a specific person rather than to "Dear Sir" or "Dear Madam." This one point will differentiate your application materials from most others. It's been my experience that about 80 percent of the folks sending in a resume will include a cover letter. Of those, only about 10 percent have gone the extra mile of bothering to find out who to send it to–that's just 8 percent of the total. And of those, at least half have misspelled either my name or the name of the employer! Misspelling a person's name is worse than not including the name at all. This means that only about 4 percent of the total number of candidates for a particular position bother to get a name and spell it right. If there are 150 people applying for one position, you would be one of six if you'd only do this. How's that for helping you to stand out!

When you call a company to ask for the name of the person who is taking the resumes, be sure to get the person's title, too. If it's an H.R. professional, ask for the name of the position's supervisor, too. Then, send in two copies of your resume, preferably with two different cover letters. Send one to the H.R. representative and one to the position's supervisor. Getting more than one copy of your application materials into the employer through various channels is a great idea because you never know which resume might end up finding the "right" person. Besides, it lets the employer know that you are serious about wanting this particular position.

There are at least two excellent reasons to write different cover letters to the same company. The first is that all the correspondence from employment candidates generally finds its way into one file. As employer representatives review your file, it'll be readily apparent to them that you merely changed names on the same letter to different people. While most people do this, wouldn't you like to be the one they see has gone the extra mile of writing something different to each person?

The second reason is that writing different letters gives you a chance to highlight different aspects of your employment or educational background.

Thus, if someone at the company is interested, she can read the various letters and get a more complete picture of who you really are.

The first paragraph of your cover letter should state the specific position for which you are applying. If you are responding to an ad, it is acceptable to attach a copy of the ad if it isn't more than about a fourth the size of the cover letter. If you have a "contact" that is relevant to this employer or position, it is good to mention the person in your initial paragraph, provided your contact has approved this. Subsequent paragraphs should cover details such as why this position and company interest you, and why you are uniquely qualified for the position.

When writing the letter, be sure to keep in mind that the company doesn't particularly care about you at this point. What they care about is what you can do to help the company. For example, instead of saying, "I'd like this job because it'll let me do all the stuff I studied while in college," try something like, "With the education and experience I gained in college, I will be able to help you reduce the amount of scrap while at the same time improving the quality of our product." Get the point? Notice the subtle use of "our product," as though the fact that they are going to hire you is already a given.

The best way to write your letter is to address specific issues that the company is currently dealing with, and, even more specifically, to address the specific issues that this particular position will be dealing with. And how do you know these issues? Check out the "Networking" and "Research" chapters.

If you can't find specifics on the company or position, then you'll have to simply cover only your qualifications. Following the introductory paragraph, you could then have one on education and certifications, and then one on relevant experience, or vice versa, depending upon which is your strong suit. Include a fourth paragraph that helps personalize the letter and then a final one to conclude the matter.

The final paragraph must put the action in your court. For example: "Mr. Smith, if I don't hear from you by Wednesday, March 14th, then I will contact you so that we can discuss this position further." Did you notice that his name was used in this sentence? Doing this helps personalize the letter and can help to increase your chances of becoming the applicant of choice.

Like all business letters, the cover letter should be typed; however, a handwritten note at the bottom does a lot to personalize it. And finally, your cover letter should only be one page long. If you can't seem to squeeze it all into such a small space, rewrite it until you can. Many job seekers have told me that their cover letters sometimes take most of a day to write because of all the editing and rewriting they have to do.

There are hundreds of books and articles that give examples of cover letters and formats, and you should refer to these if you are unsure how to write such a letter. I would, however, like to spend a little time on what you should not do. Please do not waste the reader's time with verbiage that does not make sense or that does not directly relate to the specific position for which you are applying. If your letter-writing skills aren't the best, please seek some assistance. Here are some really bad examples that employer friends of mine have received over the years.

> On behalf of my deepest personal interest, regarding the pursuit towards possible future employment consideration within your corporation, I am corresponding at this period in time to request whom it would be necessary to forward a resume of credentials, along with an appropriate address as to where I may send this information.

Good night! A simple phone call could have answered this applicant's question, and he knew the address to send this letter to, so why did he ask for an address?

Here's another bad example.

I sincerely pray that I have gained access to those resolvers who can function in synchronization in determining that I have shown sufficient flexibility in my developmental stages to be considered worthy of esteem and hire.

Who actually talks like this? For heaven's sake, write like you talk, and if you actually talk like this get someone else to write your letter.

Here's a third bad example.

I would like to introduce myself. My name is John Doe. I am from Lincoln, NE and am currently living in Cheyenne, WY. I am 36 years old and have three daughters (two from a previous marriage).

The fact that this applicant wanted to introduce himself is obvious, so it doesn't need to be stated. That's the whole purpose of a cover letter. The applicant's name should have been above his address, which this guy didn't bother to include in his cover letter, and in the signature line. Therefore he didn't need to state his name in the body of the letter.

Employers don't need to know where he's from, and had he put his address on his cover letter like he should have, he wouldn't have had to say where he's currently living. Finally, his age and family situation had absolutely nothing to do with his qualifications for the job.

Here's a fourth example.

You may have an interest in reviewing my credentials. I hope so.

"You may?"…"I hope so." Both of these phrases made the applicant seem very insecure. Applicants need to be more assertive to increase their chances of success.

Each of the above four examples were the first paragraphs on the cover letters. Not one of these applicants made it past the initial screener to the next stage in the process! The point is, how you write your cover letters is very important, so choose your words carefully.

Chapter Eleven

Employment Applications

An application is one of those things that is so basic that people think they know everything there is to know about them. After reviewing thousands of them over the years, let me tell you that they are not so basic, and a lot of people make a lot of mistakes with them.

To begin with some real basics, when you get an application from an employer, ask for two so you have an extra in case you make an error. When filling it out, make sure you write neatly and legibly and spell correctly. Also, be sure to have complete information. If the form asks for the name and address of your previous employer and you only put the name, this does not impress the person reviewing your information. If you don't know the exact street or mailing address, at the very least include the city and state. Finally, don't put "See Resume." Fill out every space on the application that asks for information.

Always fill out the application in blue or black ink because not only does it look more professional, but it lasts longer, too. Sometimes applications are shuffled quite a bit, or filed away for a while, and pencil marks simply wear off. In such cases, when the employer is finally ready to review the application, it could end up taking more work than it is worth.

Be sure to read the instructions before filling the application out. Some specifically ask that you not leave any gaps of time unaccounted for. In these cases, be sure to leave no gaps. If your employment stopped for some reason because you returned to school or became a homemaker, for example, be sure to indicate what you did during that time. Furthermore, most applications ask that you account for your time in reverse order, with what you are currently doing first. If this is how the employer wants it, be absolutely certain that you provide it this way.

Whenever possible, don't fill out the application at the place you're applying. But, if you must fill it out there, be sure to have all the necessary information with you. The best way to do this is to carry along a "master application." This is a completed application that contains correct dates, addresses, phone numbers and area codes, and spellings of names. Then, simply copy the information from your master application onto the current application.

It is extremely important to make sure your dates are correct. I have interviewed many people who were rejected for positions because they couldn't explain what they were doing for months or years at a time. And, make certain that your resume, application, and what you say in the interview all match. Several times I've interviewed people whose resumes indicated they worked somewhere for two years, for example, and the application indicated five years.

When possible, try to get the application from, and turn it in to, the manager herself. This way you'll be able to introduce yourself and she'll have a face to put with your name. This can be especially important for entry-level positions and for smaller employers. Sometimes the person sitting at the front desk might have a friend or family member applying for the same position. If you turn your application in to this person, it might never find its way to the manager.

The way to get it to the manager is to find out his name and then ask for him by name when you walk in. To do this you can either call ahead to ask, or you can ask the receptionist when you first walk in. Either way, you'll then want to simply ask, "Is Joe Smith available?" Asking like this will send the subtle message that you know the manager personally, and greatly increase the chance that the receptionist will get the manager for you.

Make the most of the opportunity to present yourself on the application and use all the space available to you. But, make sure you do so neatly. Don't crowd too much information into each space, and avoid writing in the margins.

You shouldn't leave any blanks on an application. If a particular question is not relevant to your situation, then put "N/A" (Not Applicable), or a simple slash or dash mark. This way, you indicate that you did not simply overlook the question.

If you would rather answer a particular question in person, simply say so on the application rather than leaving it blank. For example, if one of the questions is "If you were ever fired, please explain why," you could simply say, "will gladly discuss in an interview."

The only part of an application I would ever recommend leaving blank is the salary information, but even then, you could write something like "competitive wage/salary." To learn why, read the "Salary Negotiation" chapter.

Don't make the mistake of putting "fuzzy information" on the Job History section of the application. Examples of this include a computer operator not indicating software packages that he is familiar with, a journeyman machinist not indicating which machines she has used, a typist not listing her typing speed, or a human resource specialist not indicating which employment laws he is knowledgeable of. If you indicate that you are experienced in a particular field, it generally works to your advantage to list some specifics so you can subliminally prove your expertise.

I mention that not doing so could be a mistake because there might be times when you would actually want to leave such information out. For example, if you are that computer operator, and in your research on the company you've learned that it uses different software than what you've used, then you might not want to list the specific packages you are familiar with. Doing so could highlight the fact that there would be a learning curve to get you up to speed on the company's software. This is one reason that you should do some research and networking on any employer that you are hoping to work for.

After completing the application, be sure to reread it thoroughly, word-for-word and date-for-date, to catch any errors. Having to explain or apologize during the interview (if you overlooked something or made a mistake) does not make you look good.

Before turning in the application, make a copy for yourself. This way, you will have something to remind yourself of what you said and how you said it. If you're mailing it in, be sure to include a letter of application if you're doing so without a resume, or a cover letter if you're submitting a resume at the same time. If you're dropping it off, it's best to actually hand it to someone, as opposed to merely setting it on a stack in the Human Resource Department's lobby.

Chapter Twelve

Job Search Research

While conducting a job search, three types of research are extremely important for you to do.

The first is research on employers. This would obviously include any employer with which you are pursuing employment. It can also, however, include other employers. For example, you should research the competitors of the employer you are interested in working for. It can also be wise to study employers that are geographically located close to your employer of choice because you might learn of issues that are relevant to employers in that particular neighborhood. And, of course, if your employer of choice is a subsidiary of another company, or owns subsidiaries, you should study the "parent" or "child" companies, too.

These days, the Internet, is one of the best ways, if not *the* best way, to obtain information on employers. Most have a web site with an address similar to the name of the company, such as: www.nameofcompany.com. Of course, the site is just that—it's the company's. As such, it shares the perspective of how the company sees itself, or how it wants to be seen. This is a perspective that you need to be aware of. It's also a good idea to go elsewhere on the Internet to see how others view the employer in question.

If you hope to learn about a publicly held company, you'll want to get a copy of its most recent annual report. Actually, you should get several years' worth of these annual reports so you can read how the company has grown (or shrunk) over the years. You can always get these from the company itself and can sometimes get them from your local public library.

Most employers have other information about themselves that you can get from them. This other information could include publicity materials, product or service advertisements, and recruiting brochures, just to name a few. A visit to the company's Public Relations office should set you up with a lot of good information. And anything you can get will help.

Your public library is a good place to get information on employers. If you're not well-versed on where to look, or what to look for, ask a librarian for assistance. Some specific materials you could ask for include: Directory of Corporate Affiliations; Dunn and Bradstreet's Middle Market Dictionary; Encyclopedia of Associations, Vol. 1, National Organizations; The Foundation Dictionary; Moody's Industrial Manual; (state) Manufacturing Directory; Dunn and Bradstreet's Reference Book of Corporate Management; and magazines and newspapers featuring local business interests.

The local Chamber of Commerce is another great source of information. It can provide you with free general information on organizations as well as lists of manufacturers and processors. Other listings and brochures are usually available for free also.

Other places to get information on employers include the following: the Better Business Bureau, the telephone book, the people in your network and at whatever professional association meetings you attend, your local Job Service, and career counselors at local schools (try both the local high schools as well as any colleges).

To learn about a company's work environment, there are a couple of tricks you can use. One is to park outside the employee exit and watch employees leaving. Do they shuffle out like they've been beaten all day long, or do they skip out with smiles on their faces? Are they chatting effortlessly with each other or are they walking as though they were islands unto themselves? This is also a good opportunity to check out how they dress, which will provide you with clues to the company's culture.

Another trick is to sit at the counter of a nearby coffee shop. Strike up a conversation with someone next to you and you might be lucky enough to discover that it's someone who works for the employer you want to learn about. If you can't do this with another customer, try the waitress. You can bet she hears all the gossip that the employees talk about. She'll be able to tell you whether they grumble a lot or are happy as a whole. She will also be able to tell you if there is some sort of current issue that has them all concerned.

Here's an example of how research paid off for a client of mine. The ad she replied to had mentioned preference for a master's degree and three to five years of related experience. She had a bachelor's degree (with a very low G.P.A.) and absolutely no experience. She later discovered that more than 300 people, most of whom met the qualifications, had applied for the position. Yet she was hired. Why? One of the reasons was the research she did.

She had spent at least 20 hours researching that company. It was an exciting company and the more she learned about it, the more she was interested in the position. This interest level showed itself during the interviews and was actually contagious. I know, because she told me that many months after getting the job, the man who hired her shared that after he'd interviewed her he was more excited than he had ever been to be working at that company.

During her initial interview, when the interviewer asked what she knew about the company, she shared details that even he didn't know. And she kept sharing until he had to say, "enough!" (with an astonished smile). Furthermore, when it came time for her to ask questions, she asked a couple that he couldn't answer. But that shouldn't be your goal. Your goal when asking questions should simply be to let the interviewer know, without having to say it, that you've done your homework. By doing this, when you say you want to work for the company, the interviewer knows you really mean it.

Another way to get some good information on employers is from the local newspaper. Many papers now allow you to search their archives via the Internet. If you are not comfortable with computers, you can review old copies at the newspaper office, or for a small fee the paper will generally do a search for you. Using the Internet or having the paper do it for you is especially beneficial if you are attempting to research an employer in another area because you can get all the information you need without ever leaving your house.

One time, for example, a small company in Alaska invited one of my clients up there for an interview. My client simply called that town's local newspaper and asked it to do a search for him. Specifically, he asked the newspaper to go back three years and pull up any articles dealing with that employer, its administrator, union activities, and a few other key words that might shed some light on the employer. It cost him about $40 (not to mention a few long distance phone calls), but when he got up there for the interview he knew what was going on.

There really is an unlimited amount of information that you could learn about any employer. Here's a basic list of questions you should find answers to before you have an interview.

- What is the name of the company? (This may seem pretty basic, but it isn't to some people. Unbelievably, when I worked at a manufacturer in Texas, about 25 percent of the applicants pluralized the first word of the manufacturer's name, or wrote "Company" instead of "Corporation." A small matter to me, but not to some of our executives!)
- What does the firm do?
- How long has the company been in business?
- Where are its plants, stores, or offices?
- What has been its growth? (stock, employees, distribution, etc.)
- How do its prospects look for the future?

- Do the company's products or services have a long-term market?
- Who is in charge of the company?
- What culture does it promote?
- Who is in charge of the department that you would be working for?
- Who are the competitors?
- How many competitors are in the field?
- Are they large or small? (Know some numbers.)
- What makes the company's services or products distinctive?
- What would your responsibilities be?
- Who has hiring authority?
- What is the recent movement of the company's stock (if it is a publicly held corporation)? This includes knowing how the stock is doing on the day of the interview.

The second type of research you should conduct is on your industry or field. Most professions have a body of knowledge that surrounds them, and this body of knowledge is constantly growing. If you are not working, you have a unique opportunity to keep up with this ever-evolving body of knowledge.

More than likely, the people interviewing you don't have this luxury, so if you are current on what's happening in your field, you will seem especially knowledgeable. The field of information technology is an excellent example. New technologies are constantly being developed, and existing technologies are constantly being revised and changed. If you're not working, spend some of your time staying current on the changes in your field. You'll have more time now than you ever will when actually holding down a job!

Research on your industry or field also deals with studying trends. By studying these trends, you may be able to develop your own observations that are unique. Sharing such observations during interviews can show employers that you have a mind of your own and that you are not afraid to use it!

Of course, you wouldn't want to share anything outlandish. This can certainly hurt you more than help you. If you're not sure whether your ideas are odd, share them with some of the contacts in your network. This will give you a good opportunity to remind them that you are still pursuing employment and could help to prevent you from sharing something in an interview that would be detrimental to you.

If the type of work you do has little to do with the employer's actual product, service, or industry (such as a security guard hoping to work for a computer manufacturer), you might care less about the two types of research mentioned thus far. If this describes you, then all that can be said is that if you want the job, you'd better start to care! This book is not just for high-level management types of people. Employers want intelligent employees who are interested in their product or service, and who know the industry, at all levels within the organization.

At some point in the interview process you will probably be asked two questions: "What do you know about the company?" and "Do you have any questions?" By doing some proper research, your response to these questions can definitely determine whether you get the job.

This is a good place to mention one of the differences between older employment candidates and younger ones. I can't tell you the number of times I've interviewed older candidates who had no answer to those two questions when I asked them. Meanwhile, their younger competitors often responded in a way that demonstrated that they had gone the extra mile in their effort to get the job.

Which person would you want to hire? The one who just sat back and trusted in his vast amount of experience, or the one who showed he was willing to do whatever it took to get the job? Older candidates have a major advantage over younger ones when they not only trust in their past experience, but show that they are willing to be future-oriented, too.

Of course, this difference between older candidates and younger ones can be related to every other aspect of the job search, not just to research. Older candidates have so much to offer and really are the employee of choice more often than they think. However, they must be as aggressive in their job searches as their younger counterparts.

The third and final type of research you need to do is learn how to conduct a job search. The fact that you're reading this book shows that you have already discovered the importance of this. However, don't let it stop here. The Internet is a phenomenal resource for job search tips and information. And, as mentioned previously, there are hundreds of published books and articles on nearly every aspect of the job search. Any areas you are not particularly comfortable with deserve your further attention.

Chapter Thirteen

Networking

A favorite networking example of mine has to do with a client named Gene. When Gene decided to relocate to another part of the country, the only people he knew there were his sister and her husband. Neither was in his line of work and neither was in a position to introduce him to anybody that could help in his job search. Within two weeks he had developed an excellent network and had contacts within various companies around the area.

The first thing Gene did was determine who the 10 largest employers in the area were, as well as who their hiring managers were. He then contacted these people and asked to meet with them. Eight out of the 10 agreed to meet with him, and two of those meetings turned into actual interviews! To learn how he established who they were, read the rest of this chapter and then the "Research" chapter, if you haven't yet read it. To learn how he actually got those folks to meet with him, read the rest of this chapter carefully.

The second thing Gene did was personally visit every temporary agency in the area. There were a lot of them and he did this even though he had absolutely no interest in working for a temporary agency! Why would he go to the effort of personally visiting all of them? The answer is simple: His field was Human Resources. As an H.R. professional, he knew that the managers of those agencies were in daily contact with H.R. departments as well as with employers who needed H.R. departments.

Gene's sister had lived in that city for half a decade, and his brother-in-law had lived in the area his entire life, yet in two weeks he knew more people in more companies than they did. And this was just the beginning of his networking activities. It was the foundation from which all his other efforts were made successful. For example, when he attended the next luncheon for H.R. professionals, he knew several people, and since they knew his situation, they were only too happy to introduce him to associates of theirs who had open positions!

Networking is one of the most important aspects, if not *the* most important aspect, of your job search. To be truly successful you must do it, and you must do it intelligently and purposefully.

Networking is not merely telling everybody you meet that you are looking for employment. It's about making friends in the professional world. People don't just want to hear about your problems and what you want, and you must keep this in mind when networking or your attempts will work against you more than for you.

One thing that most people love to do is talk about their personal opinions and ideas. They don't mind offering suggestions if they believe that the person receiving the suggestion will actually think it's of value. So a lot of networking is letting other people share their thoughts. And while you definitely don't want to come across as a yes man, agreeing blindly with every wild idea, you do want to be selective about what you disagree with.

A lot of the strategy of networking is to convince people that you sincerely want to learn from their experience. The way to do this is to be truly sincere about your desire to learn. Isn't that a neat little trick—the way to convince them that you are sincere is to actually be sincere!

If you are a proud individual who feels that you already know it all, then networking may not work well for you. However, since you are out looking for work, I would hope that you realize that you can learn from others. After all, even if they are half your age, they have different experiences and educational knowledge than you and they do have something to offer.

Therefore, be open to what they have to say. And besides, listening to them will impress them that you are exceedingly intelligent. Why? Because they'll think that if you are smart enough to listen to them then you must be smart! Respecting what they have to say will win you over to them, and then next time they hear about an opening, guess who they'll call?

With the preceding paragraphs as an introduction to this subject, let's now turn our attention to where you can find these people that you want to listen to.

Certainly one of the best places to start is with any professional association related to your field. If you are already a member, great! Now become an active member. Attend all the meetings and volunteer for any committees that interest you. And remember what I said about folks not wanting to hear only about your situation. Talk with them, learn about what's happening in their workplace, and if you can offer some choice suggestions, go for it. Then, when the opportunity presents itself, go ahead and let them know that you are looking for a job.

When you attend these meetings, position yourself to your best advantage. For example, if you see a key player sitting at a table on the other side of the room, find a way to sit at the same table if at all possible. However, it's generally best to do this subtly. If you just barge over and bark out that you want to sit there to get to know so-and-so, you will appear to lack good taste. Instead, I recommend that you just happen to find yourself there, and use the conversation at the table to get acquainted with the person you want to meet.

Relationships with those key players are usually best when nurtured over time. When you attend a meeting, be sure to have nothing planned for several hours after it's scheduled to be over. This way, if you end up getting invited somewhere after the meeting, you will be able to take advantage of the opportunity. And, of course, you should arrive early to each meeting to take advantage of any networking opportunities beforehand.

Cold calling can be a great networking tool, too. This is how Gene managed to get into eight of the 10 largest employers within his first two weeks of looking for employment in his new city. Two things must be done before attempting this. First, you'll need to do a little research to determine which employers you want to target. And remember, if your target audience is too large, it'll end up bogging you down and prevent you from actively pursuing real opportunities.

Here's an example to show you what I mean. When Gene got to his new city he could have decided to find out who the 200 largest employers were. However, had he done that he wouldn't have been able to call any of them for several weeks because it would have taken that long just to research who they were, who the hiring managers were, and what the managers' direct telephone numbers were. So to keep it simple, he decided upon 10. It could have been 12, 15 or even 20. The point is, he started with a manageable number and could later expand his scope if necessary and if time allowed.

Once you know specifically whom to call, you need a strategy to deal with the most likely objections. In Gene's case, he knew that most H.R. departments are extremely busy. This means that they don't have much time to give to someone they don't know. Furthermore, he knew that when he got in touch with them, their primary objection to seeing him (other than not having time) would be that they didn't have any openings.

Therefore, when he called, he had a 15-second opening that took away both objections. Specifically, he said, "Hi! My name is Gene Smith and I'm an H.R. professional who's new to the area. While I realize that you probably don't have any openings right now, I'd sure appreciate it if we could meet just briefly so I could learn a bit about the local market. Being an H.R. professional myself, I know you're busy, so I promise not to take up more than five minutes of your time."

Since he had covered both possible objections in his introduction, eight out of the 10 H.R. managers agreed to see him. One kept him in the lobby, but the rest invited him up to their offices.

One thing that is tremendously important is that if you make a promise to anybody in your network, you must keep it. A specific example from Gene's case was the fact that he had promised to only take five minutes of time with the H.R. professionals. When he met with these folks, he'd look at his watch and after five minutes he'd stand up and say, "Excuse me, I'm sorry but my time is up." This was usually done while they were still talking, as he was there to listen to them.

I don't think that a single one of them actually allowed him to leave at that point, but when they invited him to stay a bit longer, he was staying at their invitation.

And just like the time you allow yourself before and after a professional association meeting, be sure to have nothing planned for several hours after the scheduled five-minute meeting. You want to make yourself available in case you get the chance to speak with other people in the company. Therefore, you should only schedule two networking meetings a day–one first thing in the morning and one in the early afternoon.

When you meet with these folks, remember that it's your meeting. Since you asked for it, you need to come with an agenda. Specifically, have three to five good, solid questions prepared that you can ask their opinions on. You definitely don't want these to be basic questions that anyone would know the answer to. It's best if your questions are based on a current issue from their business, the local market, or a publication related to your field.

At the end of any initial networking meeting, be sure to ask if you can keep in touch. This again shows you respect their time. Also, you don't want to keep in touch too often lest you become a bother. A good approach is generally to alternate between a letter and a phone call–one about every two weeks.

The week after the H.R. manager met with Gene, the manager received a thank you letter. About two weeks later, Gene called and chatted for a few minutes, being sure that he had something specific to ask so the H.R.

manager didn't feel that his time was being wasted. Two weeks after that, Gene sent another brief note, and so on.

At the end of the initial meeting, always ask the person you're meeting with if he'd accept a copy of your resume to keep on file, just in case he hears of something. And then each time you write, include a fresh copy—just in case he misplaced the last one.

As you read above, Gene's strategy for employers that he might actually want to work for was to call ahead and set up an appointment. For the temporary agencies, however, he simply walked in and asked to speak to the managers. One of the main reasons for this difference is the fact that most temporary agencies only employ five to 10 people, so Gene figured it wouldn't be as difficult to get in to see the managers (not as many hallways, security checks, and the like).

The point of the two different approaches is that he considered the two different types of businesses involved and then decided how to proceed. Please note, he did not just sit back and wait for them to call him. For your job search to be successful, you need to take charge of it. The simple fact of the matter could be that it might have been a mistake to just charge into the temp agencies without setting up an appointment. Maybe a smarter person would have called first. But most people wouldn't have called and wouldn't have gone in person. Fact is, most people simply don't pursue a professional network like they should. If getting the job you want depended on it, wouldn't you rather take the risk of making a slight faux pas than not acting at all?

By the way, those two networking meetings that turned into interviews for Gene were both for unadvertised positions! That's one of the beauties of networking—you get the "inside scoop" on positions that other folks who only look in the newspaper never hear about. It's common knowledge in the field of recruiting that more than 80 percent of open positions are never advertised!

When you contact an employer, you should set up a network with both the H.R. personnel and with personnel within the department that's related to your field. For example, if you are an engineer, you should set up a network with both H.R. people and folks from the Engineering Department. If you are a buyer, you should do so with H.R. people and folks from the Purchasing Department, and so on.

There is, however, one important thing to keep in mind regarding the order in which you contact these folks. Most companies prefer you to work through the H.R. Department, so if you contact it first, and someone asks you not to contact a manager directly, then you are limiting yourself. Of course, you could decide to ignore the request and contact the manager anyway, but this generally gets back to the H.R. representative and then she might decide to work against you.

Therefore, you should contact people within the particular department that you hope to work before contacting the H.R. people. This way, when you do contact H.R., and when someone asks you not to establish any contacts with folks elsewhere in the company, you will already have made your contacts. And even people in H.R. can't expect you not to call friends who have already been established.

One very important thing to keep in mind is that anybody can be part of your network. After all, you never know who knows who, and it's certainly possible that an engineer friend could put in a good word to the H.R. Department when you are applying for a purchasing position!

What's more, networking isn't just for making contacts that can introduce you to hiring managers. Network contacts are also good sources for information about new industries and fields that you may want to pursue. Remember that anyone you meet could be the contact that ends up helping you get the job you're after.

One thing all of us should keep in mind when networking is that the people we end up getting in touch with might be afraid we're after their jobs. Be sensitive to this, and either relieve them of their fears if this is not the case, or pursue someone further up the chain of command if it is true.

One excellent source of people for your network are the folks that interview you for jobs. Just think about it. These folks thought enough of you to invite you in for an interview, and they know your qualifications about as good as anyone because they spent time interviewing you.

If they end up not selecting you for their positions, simply add them to your network. Most people who try this, however, foul it up miserably. The reason for this is that they can't seem to get past the fact that they weren't hired. Every time they call, the interviewer cringes at the thought of having to talk to them because of the questions they ask: Why wasn't I hired? How can I improve my interview technique? Are you recommending me to any other departments? etc.

Before asking these kinds of questions, try placing yourself in their shoes. Most interviewers would love to help you out for future interviews. However, some people will sue a company for any reason whatsoever. Since we live in such a "sueciety," companies have had to establish policies to keep interviewers from sharing opinions, advice, and reasons for hiring decisions with interviewees. So when you ask an interviewer for such an opinion, it immediately sets up an internal struggle where she can't do what she'd like to do, which is to share some techniques to help you in future interviews.

Here is a specific example of a similar situation from an employer friend of mine. He interviewed a young woman and didn't recommend her for further interviews, so the woman, who happened to be the niece of one of the company's managers, didn't get the job. Awhile after the interview, her aunt (the manager) asked my friend what the woman could have done differently. Because he was speaking to a manager, and because my friend has the natural desire to help people, he went ahead and answered her question, which was against company policy. The next day, the manager told my friend that her niece had cried for hours upon hearing the critique of her interview. It made my friend feel terrible because all he'd wanted to do was to help.

Don't do that to the folks who interview you. Once you know that you have not been selected for a position, call them up and let them know that you understand that they were able to find a better match, and (sincerely) wish them the best. Then ask them to keep you in mind for any other openings that they might have. You never know–the person who was selected might not report to work or might not be a good fit for the job, and if you've properly maintained this contact, you could very well be next in line!

If, for some reason, the interviewer does tell you why you weren't hired, don't argue with him or make him justify his answers. Instead, thank him for his advice and work on developing him as network contact for future employment opportunities.

As you build your network, always ask your contacts if they can think of anyone else you should call. And be sure to remember their names. It'd be awful if you saw them unexpectedly and couldn't say hello properly.

Let's move on and look at some other avenues to build your network. One of these could be miscellaneous luncheons, breakfasts, and dinners. When conducting a real job search, you must mingle with people. Attend whatever meetings you can where there's even the slightest possibility of meeting someone who could either help you or might know someone else that could.

Here are other ideas:

- Make contacts with people in related businesses.
- Make sure all your professional contacts, family, friends, and casual acquaintances are aware of your search.
- Keep in touch with Job Service personnel and other public assistance offices.
- Develop relationships with a few professors at the local university.

Your job is to know what you have to offer, have a positive "can-do" attitude, and have a few short success stories ready to share. Always have quality resumes to hand out, and be open and ready for any opportunity. That, my friend, is networking in a nutshell!

An excellent book on basic people skills that will help you in your net-working attempts is *How to Win Friends and Influence People* by Dale Carnegie.

Chapter Fourteen

Resumes

This is a subject on which there really are volumes of material. As part of your research you should get a couple of the many books available on this topic–your local library will have several. These books will help you decide which format will work best for you, as well as the best wording to use.

Here are some basic points to remember:

- One page is best, two is a maximum (for the initial "screening" resume).
- Use heavy, quality paper.
- Use only one side of the paper.
- Make good use of margins and spacing–don't let it look cluttered.
- Use a type size that is readable; 12 point is preferred. Don't use anything smaller than 10 point.
- Spell everything correctly.
- Avoid photocopied resumes. Provide an original printout whenever possible.

To design the heading of your resume, center your name, in large print (14 or 16 point), at the top of the page on a line by itself. On the next two lines, left-justify your address, and right-justify your phone number with area code. If at all possible, be sure to include an e-mail address, too. This will leave your name in the center by itself. This way as the resume reviewer is looking at your resume, she constantly sees your name. If your address and phone number are directly under your name, then it will be hidden in a block of text and you won't end up with the same amount of name recognition as you'd get otherwise.

I generally recommend a thick solid line directly under your address and phone number. This line goes from margin to margin, and leaves space under it before beginning the Objective. Having such a line separates the top information from the body of your resume. This creates a letterhead look that is neat, clean, and professional. Here are two examples of how it could look.

Your Name

| Street/Mailing Address | Phone Number |
| City, State ZIP code | E-mail Address |

Your Name

Street/Mailing Address	Home Phone Number
City, State ZIP code	Work Phone Number
Home E-mail Address	Work E-mail Address

If your name is difficult to pronounce, employers appreciate your including your nickname in parentheses or quotation marks. For example, I once hired a guy whose first name was Kitsitbumrung. On his resume, he indicated that he went by "Sit." This certainly made it easier on all of us in the interview loop!

Always use an Objective or Summary statement (for most, an Objective is best). This should be directly under your name and address. Make absolutely certain that your objective actually says something. My all-time favorite bad example is a five-line objective I once saw that went as follows:

> To use my experience and skills to secure a position where there are challenges, and where advancement increases with my abilities. And to work with other highly motivated personnel for the attainment of corporate goals.

The problem with this is that we don't have any idea what type of employment this person wants. Is he an accountant? An engineer? A coal miner? We simply don't know. Because corporate resume reviewers learn to skim resumes in just a few seconds, this guy's time would be up and his resume would be put in the "no" pile. Sure, he might have been qualified, but he couldn't focus. He didn't know how to make the most out of the short opportunity available to him. Lines to an Objective are like pages to a resume: One is best, two is maximum.

Not all professions require a resume. In some blue-collar professions, such as construction and mechanic related fields, a resume might do more to draw suspicion than to help you get the job. The rule here is to do whatever is normal in your industry. If you don't know what's normal in your industry, ask someone in your network.

Never include date or place of birth, Social Security number, marital status, number of children, a picture, or other personal information that has nothing to do with your qualifications for a job. A real-life example that I once received from a woman applying for a position at a telecommunications corporation said the following: "Married with two children: ages three years old (twins)." Unless she was applying for a position at a school or day care facility, this simply was not relevant.

Don't put your references on your resume. Use a separate sheet of paper, and to tie the two together (as well as to make your application materials look especially professional and well-organized), use the same typestyle, paper, and letterhead for both documents.

As a matter of fact, if you're looking for something to cut on your resume, take off the "References available upon request" statement. Most resumes end with this useless little piece of non-information. It simply is not needed. If you want the job, and if references are necessary, of course you'd make them available upon request.

Realizing that most resumes (in other words, your competition) end with that bland statement, consider ending your resume with something a bit more exciting. This gives resume reviewers something unique and solid to help them remember you over the others. It acts as a hook that might help draw them back to your resume.

Customize your resume. For example, I am a Human Resource generalist. This means that I have experience in recruitment (job selection and placement), employee and labor relations, compensation and benefits, training and development, and management practices.

I have one resume that shows me off as a generalist–its objective points to a generalist position and the "meat" of the resume gives equal space to each of the various disciplines within my field. However, because a lot of employers break their H.R. departments up into the various specializations, I also have a recruiter resume, and another that highlights my training experience. Both of these specialization resumes show that I am a generalist, but their objectives point to the particular specialization I am highlighting.

Customization can, of course, be taken much more seriously than this. Specifically, you can and should customize your resume for each position that you apply for. If you're responding to a newspaper ad, this will allow you to use the specific words in the ad. Furthermore, it'll allow you to speak to specifics within the particular employer to which you are applying.

Basically, your one-to two-page resume is the one you should send initially; however, it is acceptable to have an expanded resume with you when you go in to an interview. The expanded resume can be of any length (typically two to six pages long) and provides much more detail as to what you've done in your various employment experiences as well as all your academic credentials and any other relevant information.

If you are out of work, it's wise to work for yourself in your field while conducting your job search, either for compensation or on a volunteer basis. By doing this, your resume can show a current employer related to your field. This way, employers won't be so concerned that your knowledge, skills, and abilities are getting old. It is also a good time to write and publish some articles or even a book about your field. You can bet that this would look good to prospective employers when they ask what you've been doing with your time!

Working for yourself can also help you overcome an employer's natural tendency to want to hire someone who's currently employed. Employers typically think that if people have something to offer, then they'd be employed by someone, somewhere. So if you're not employed, especially for an extended period of time, it could cause some employers to be hesitant to hire you.

In all the thousands of resumes that I've seen, there's one idea I've seen used only twice. It is to have a cover sheet to the resume. Unlike a cover letter that tries to say and do a whole slew of things, a cover sheet is mostly blank, except for a small part that is smartly centered and does nothing more than introduce the resume with a bit of a flare.

The first one I saw was from a lady in the New England states. Stapled on top of her resume was a blank sheet that had the following words printed inside a nice border:

PLEASE!!
Take a few minutes
and get to know
an exceptional person!!

Sue Smith

This impressed me because it was original. After reviewing about 200 resumes, it was a nice break to see something refreshingly different. Of course, this wouldn't work for everyone. It is important that however you present your application material is consistent with your personality, the type of job that you are after, and the corporate culture of the particular employer you are applying to.

The second example was from a young man in California. He attached his resume to a sheet of paper that was a copy of a short article (one column by three inches) indicating that he had qualified for the Olympics. Above this article, he'd typed out the following: Introducing John Doe

While the article really didn't have much to do with the job he was applying for, it was especially noteworthy (as opposed to where you were born or how many children you have). Furthermore, employers like to hire "winners" as well as healthy people with ambition, and having qualified for the Olympics certainly spoke to those things.

As you develop your resume, there are a couple of things to remember. First of all, it's not what it is, but what it does. In other words, you don't just want it to look nice, you want it to be your ticket into interviews. No matter how nice it looks, if you're not getting interviews, your resume is one of the first things you should look at. A resume won't get you a job. The resume's job is to open doors and get you interviews.

The other thing to keep in mind is that everything on your resume should answer the question "So what?" No matter how wonderful the education or experience is that you want to put on your resume, if it isn't relevant to the job you are after, then it doesn't belong.

Chapter Fifteen

Transferable Skills

One client spent a year working in the underground coal mines of Pennsylvania. His very next job was an office job as a purchasing agent for an international corporation and had nothing to do with fossil fuels. How did he manage to switch from one field to another so drastically different? A big part of the answer is in how he used his transferable skills.

Transferable skills are those skills that are used in one profession that can be transferred to another. There were few, if any, "hard" or technical skills that he could transfer from the coal mine job to the office job. There were, however, several "soft" or intrinsic skills that would transfer.

After carefully analyzing both jobs to see what traits the one had that the other needed, we determined that my client had these skills to transfer:

1. He was a fast learner.
2. He could take responsibility.
3. He could handle stress.
4. He could work with diverse types of people.

Each of these were skills that the purchasing agent job required, and he had specific examples of using these same skills when he worked at the coal mine.

During the interviews for the purchasing agent job, whenever interviewers asked my client about what he did at the coal mine, he did not go into all the detail about his daily tasks. These tasks weren't related to the job he wanted, and therefore the interviewers really weren't interested in them. Instead, my client explained how he had never seen a transit before in his life, yet within about two months he was going underground and directing miners around gas wells and other dangerous situations.

He then explained how this demonstrated the fact that he was a fast learner (the first transferable skill). When he went on to explain that if he had made a mistake there could have been an explosion that would have killed over a dozen men, it demonstrated his ability to take responsibility (the second transferable skill).

Continuing on, he shared the fact that the miners were paid by the amount of coal they mined, and when he was surveying the face of the mine, he'd have to get them all to stop working for however long it would take him to do his work. They never appreciated this and would sit in a circle around him. Before long they'd be throwing insults his way. If he didn't finish up shortly after this started, he'd soon be hearing threats and cursing. The fact that he was able to make it through all this showed that he was able to handle stress (the third transferable skill), and could work with diverse types of people (the fourth transferable skill).

In addition to showing these four transferable skills, he was able to use the coal mine job to his advantage in two other ways. For one, it showed that he wasn't afraid of "real" work—you know, the type of work where you actually get your hands dirty! The other way had to do with the fact that he had been laid off because of a unionization attempt. Because of this, he didn't think much of unions—and the employer he was interviewing with was definitely non-union! He made sure to mention this during the interviews, and it worked to his advantage.

Use this example to determine what your transferable skills are and how to use them to your advantage. First, look at the job you want. Figure out what skills it needs, and then analyze your work experience and figure out which skills match and will transfer over. Practice telling your "transferable skills" story to make it as short and focused as possible. You don't want to bore the interviewer or have him cut you off before you finish because you haven't quickly made him understand how what you are saying relates to the position for which you are applying.

Chapter Sixteen

Addressing Your Address

If you are conducting a regional or national job search, you need to be aware of this: Many employers do their initial screen on nothing more than where you live. The basic rule of thumb is that the higher the level of the position, or the hotter the particular skills, the larger an area an employer is willing to consider candidates from. If you are in the low-to middle-income range, this could definitely work against you.

For example, if the job is in one city, and the employer gets 300 resumes for the position, the job recruiters are very likely to screen anyone out of the running who doesn't live within about an hour's drive of that city.

There are really three reasons for this. One is the fact that it helps to reduce that stack of 300 resumes. For positions in those lower-income ranges, employers generally feel that they can find local talent, so why bother looking out of the area?

Another reason might have to do with the company's affirmative action plan. While it is beyond the scope of this chapter to delve into the legalities involved, suffice it to say that certain positions are slated to be recruited for locally, while others have larger areas from which the employer can recruit.

The third reason for preferring to look locally has to do with the cost of recruiting. Most credible, legitimate, and respectable employers pay for interview trips and relocation, both of which cost money. What's more, employers are concerned with other costs, too.

One of these has to do with retention, which is a major concern to most employers. Statistics show that moving a new employee to a new area significantly reduces the chance that person will stay long-term with the company. The retention rate is affected even more if the new employee is moving a family, too. When retention goes down, recruitment costs shoot up.

Another expense employers have when relocating a new employee is the extra time it generally takes to recruit someone from out of the area. This extra time can add up to several months because of schedule conflicts, travel arrangements, packing and moving time, and time to sell the old house and buy a new one, for example. The extra time it takes to get the new employee on board represents work that isn't getting done. When work doesn't get done, it costs the employer in many ways.

So now that you know why some employers prefer to hire local people, what can you do about it? You can get a local address in whatever area the employer is located. This can end up costing you a bit of money because the employer will assume you'll pay your own expenses because you appear to be a local resident.

The best way to do this is to use a friend's or relative's address and phone number. If you don't have such contacts, the next best option is to hire the services of an answering service. This gets you both an address and a local phone number. You will, of course, need to make arrangements to get your mail and messages as soon as possible after the answering service receives them. A third option is to rent a post office box and then have your mail forwarded to you. This is the least expensive option but also the least effective because it only provides you with a local address.

Chapter Seventeen

Interviewing

You might think that a book on the proper way to conduct a job search would have several chapters explaining how to interview. And in reality, that's what has happened here. Most of what has been said throughout this book relates to how to interview!

In this chapter, however, we will get down to some specifics on this particular subject. But first, let's discuss an emotion that seems to be universally affiliated with interviewing–fear!

Most people are scared to death of interviewing. There are two major reasons for this. The first is that most of us do it rarely, don't know how to do it, and are unknowledgeable about the process. Reading this book, and this chapter specifically, will help you in this area. And, of course, the more interviews you go through, the more comfortable you will become with the process.

The second reason that most people are afraid of interviewing is that we're all naturally afraid of rejection. Something that might help you deal with this is to think about the employer's pre-interview decision, rather than the unknown post-interview decision.

The employer's decision to invite you in for an interview shows that the interviewer is already at least a little interested in what you have to offer. In other words, you've already been accepted. So rather than going to interviews wondering whether you will be accepted, go in knowing that you already have been accepted! This fact alone should do wonders for building up your confidence level!

Knowing that everybody else is as scared as you are might comfort you some, too. And another thing to keep in mind is the knowledge that while you might not be experienced at knowing how to interview, you do know what you are selling better than anybody else. Nobody knows you better than you do!

During any interview, there certainly are some basics to remember. As we discussed in previous chapters, you'll want to look your absolute best and be sure to be in control of your body language and facial expressions. You'll also want to be extremely courteous to everybody you meet during the process.

There was one time, for example, when I was doing the initial screening interview for an executive level position. The last candidate I had interviewed was the most qualified by far, and seemed extremely sharp. However, immediately after he left, our secretary, who was black, shared some comments that he made to her that demonstrated that he was prejudiced toward people of color. Hearing this, I immediately withdrew him from consideration because I knew that he wasn't the best match for our company—no matter what his qualifications were.

That man definitely knew how to interview. However, he did not know how to properly treat people before and after an interview. And this cost him the job.

Let's discuss the various types of interviews. Did you know that different interviews are used to obtain different kinds of information? If you don't understand this, then you will probably end up presenting the wrong information at the wrong time, which usually results in your being rejected.

Few companies have only one interview. If you end up interviewing with a company that does only do one interview, then you'll need to combine the advice throughout this section and present all of your various sides during that one opportunity.

However, for most of you, you will have two, three, four, and even more interviews. Some of my clients have interviewed with companies that have had two or three eight-hour days of interviews before making a hiring decision! Few of you will ever have to go through that, but if you do, the following advice is for those situations, too.

The first interview is typically with a Human Resource person. This individual verifies that everything on your application is true and checks you out to see if you would be a good fit with the company and the particular department for which you are interviewing.

During this initial interview, don't bog your answers down with too many technical details of what you did at previous employers. Keep your answers short and focused. If the interviewer wants more, she will ask. One thing to keep in mind is that initial interviews are typically used to screen people out. So don't try to stand out too much, or you might find yourself out of the running.

Typically, hourly, low-salary positions and local interviewees are handled slightly differently than the higher-paid salaried people and folks who have come in from out of the area. The main reason for this has to do with the pre-screening that is done prior to inviting someone to interview.

People in the first group are usually invited based solely on the information provided on their resumes or applications. People in the second group have generally had at least one, and maybe even two or three, phone screens before being invited to interview.

An example one employer friend shared with me has to do with hourly production employees who are typically hired from within about an hour's drive. For these folks, the employer simply reviews their applications and invites them in for interviews based on the information provided. When inviting them in, the employer tells each applicant that he is being scheduled to meet with one person. They are usually not told that any further interviews will occur. During that initial interview, the interviewer decides whether the company wants to pursue that particular candidate.

Candidates who pass the initial interview get second interviews, which vary among companies. Some arrange for the hiring supervisor to be available during the interviews so that if a good candidate is found, he can be passed on to the supervisor immediately. Others wait until all the initial candidates have been interviewed and then decide which ones to invite back in.

It is important to be aware of these possible scenarios so that when you go for an interview, you don't get frustrated if the initial interviewer avoids your questions about whether there will be further interviews.

If you do end up being screened out after the initial interview, it does not necessarily mean that all is lost. Go to the "Networking" chapter, and find out how to add the person who interviewed you to your list of network contacts. In other words, rather than harboring bad feelings toward him for having cut you, use him to your advantage.

For higher-level candidates, as well as for people coming in from out of town (especially if the employer is paying for the trip), employers usually have a full interview schedule lined up.

If an employer contacts you by telephone and begins to ask you interview-type questions, it is acceptable to suggest another time if such a time would work better for you. For example, if you are in the middle of a bad day, are rushing to meet deadlines, or have a kid bawling in the background, then you should suggest an alternate time. Telephone interviews are no different than the face-to-face ones in that you still want to put your best foot forward. You might even want to shave, shower, and dress appropriately to help you feel like you're interviewing.

Realizing that the initial interview is typically with an H.R. representative and is simply used to verify information on the application and to see if you are a fit, what are the rest of the interviews for? Further interviews will also be checking you out to see if you are a fit; however, further interviews may also be used to check out your technical skills.

Please note that I said they *may* be used to check out your technical skills. Over the years, I've discovered that some interviewers never do learn how to interview properly. For example, some of them end up doing just about all the talking during the interview.

If you are being interviewed by someone who won't let you speak, you need to simply sit back and practice your active listening skills. Interviewers will think that you are incredibly intelligent if you are smart enough to listen to the pearls of wisdom they have to offer. If, however, you continually interrupt them in an attempt to show them what you've got to offer, they won't hear you and will end up thinking that you aren't a good fit.

As previously mentioned, the initial interview or two is typically used to weed candidates out. Subsequent interviews are used to comb candidates in. Here's another way to think about this: "The first is to meet you, others are to keep you." As you get further interviews with the employer, you'll want to differentiate yourself from the other candidates. This is a better time to share your unique ideas and make suggestions–both based upon your research about the company.

How you differentiate yourself is totally up to you. But however you do it, it should be reflective of your personality and style. Here's an example of how one client did it, which resulted in the entire interview team either laughing or at least smiling big.

While being interviewed by a team of five, the interviewee was told to direct his attention to the whiteboard. In the center of it were drawn five shapes: a square, a triangle, a rectangle, a circle, and a squiggly line. Each of these shapes was about eight or 10 inches tall and wide. The interview team then asked the candidate to explain which shape was most like him; in other words, which one did he most identify with.

This was a personality test. That particular one is called Psycho-Geometrics. As the candidate looked at the whiteboard, he noticed that way up in the left-hand corner of the board was a very small mark (about an inch and a half in diameter) that he knew was NOT one of his options. He told the interviewers that he identified with that.

This, of course, begged the question "Why?" which he was able to explain. He said that he usually stood out from the crowd and came up with ideas that were unexpected and unique. He went on to say that he could usually come up with alternatives that the average professional would never think of. Hearing this, the interview team could see his point. You can bet that out of all the people the team interviewed for that position, he was the only one who chose that symbol. And you can further bet that after all the interviews, he was the person the team remembered!

Another type of interview is called the Stress Interview. Employers use this type when the position is one that will require you to be in stressful situations. Police officers and security guards, for example, shouldn't be surprised to encounter this type of interview. Everybody should be at least aware of them, though, just in case you find yourself with someone who simply likes this particular type of interview.

Typically, three to six interviewers meet with you at one time. But whether there are several, or just one, the style is basically the same. They shoot open-ended questions at you and don't give you time to think or answer completely before shooting the next question.

Since you're not given time to properly think about the questions, ask for clarification or details, and develop your answers, you are typically not very satisfied with the answers that you do give. So on top of being hit from all directions with fairly tough questions, in the back of your mind you're kicking yourself for the answers that you have given.

Other things can also be done to increase your stress level. For example, the interviewers might not smile, and quite often they'll even give you body language that is meant to tell you that you are doing a really bad job (such as frowning, shaking their heads back and forth, and taking notes in a negative sort of way). Some employers even go to the extent of raising their voices, using foul language, belittling your responses, getting "in your face," getting "personal," and other such tactics.

And that's how the whole interview goes. There might be 30 or 40 questions, and as the minutes tick by, interviewees typically get more and more flustered. Since they want the job, yet know that their answers aren't the best, it's extremely frustrating. And not only do the interviewers know this, but it's what they want!

There is, however, something you can do about it. Simply realize it for what it is and refuse to play their game! I'll share how one client handled her first stress interview to help you see one way to do this.

My client was a college student being interviewed for a resident advisor (R.A.) position in the dorms. R.A.s typically have to handle very stressful situations, so the interview team was using the stress interview as part of the screening process.

The interview team comprised eight seasoned R.A.s and directors sitting in a half-circle. My client was directed to sit in the "hot-seat," which was in the center. When the first interviewer shot his question to her, she simply shot a question back at him. He wasn't prepared for this, so he was flustered, trying to figure out whether he could or should answer. Meanwhile, the woman who was to ask the second question wasn't sure whether she should go ahead with hers. After several seconds of silence, she finally decided that she'd better ask her question. My client asked her for some clarification, and since she wasn't prepared for this, she became as flustered as the first interviewer.

The interview continued in much the same manner, and the whole time my client remained calm. Someone had told her that everyone else who had been through that interview left with sweat pouring off his forehead. But when she left, the interview team was sweating–not her! My client eventually was selected for the position, out of more than 80 original applicants!

Of course, you might not be as lucky as she was. That was a fairly inexperienced interview team that didn't know how to handle my client's responses. That trick, for example, wouldn't work if an experienced stress interviewer were conducting the proceedings.

If you're not able to do what she did, simply stick to the first rule: Remain calm, no matter what! As they shoot their questions at you, realize what they are trying to do and don't fall into their trap. That, by the way, is all they're after anyway. While they would like your answers to make sense, this is not what they are looking for. What they want to know is whether you can handle stress.

And another thing, don't smile or laugh if the questions they are presenting you with are not a laughing matter. The interviewers not only want to see *whether* you can handle stress, but they also want to see *how* you handle stress. Laughter is one of the natural tension releases that God has equipped us with, but in certain stressful situations it might not be appropriate.

Here's an important final note on stress interviews. Make certain that it is a stress interview before you set out to thwart their attempts to frustrate you. For example, just because it's a five-person interview team doesn't always mean that you're going into a stress interview situation. If the interviewers remain calm and relaxed and are allowing you time to think and the opportunity to ask questions, then handle it as a regular interview. Otherwise, you could look pretty silly and end up not being considered further for the position.

The order in which you are interviewed can be very important. To be the last one interviewed for a position is best, and if you can't be last, the next best position is to be first. The reasons are fairly basic. If you're the last, they'll remember you the best. If you're the first, then you're the one that they'll be comparing everyone else to.

There are a couple of tricks to help you position yourself. When the interviewers call you, ask when they are doing their interviews. They will typically say something like, "We're hoping to finish them up by next Wednesday." If that's the case, indicate that the best time for you is as late on Wednesday as possible. If they indicate a morning or early afternoon time, ask if there's anything later, or what about Thursday morning?

Another trick is to use your answering machine to your advantage. It is possible to push your interview out a whole week by simply playing "phone tag." For example, if a recruiter calls you on a Tuesday, it's fairly reasonable for him to expect you to be available for an interview by that Friday. If, however, you had let your answering machine take that Tuesday call, and then you returned the call Wednesday late afternoon, he wouldn't see it as unreasonable when you request that the interview be the following week.

Games? Yes, but you can bet the recruiter is scheduling the interviews when they'll work out best for him, so why not do the same thing for yourself–to your advantage. However, you do not want to lose an interview opportunity (or the job) over this. In reality, you need to make yourself available whenever the employer wants you to be available. So be careful, and only push your luck as much as you can without overdoing it. If you sense that the employer is about to make a hiring decision, for example, then you need to interview as soon as possible.

Another example of playing the game to your advantage is if the recruiter indicates that a later interview time is acceptable, but it will mean that you wouldn't get to meet with one or two members of the interview team. In such a case, do whatever is necessary to get an interview while they are all available. You never know which ones might be holding the strings to make the final hiring decision.

I must mention one final thing before moving on to how to answer specific questions: Honesty. You have to be honest. This does not mean that you have to hurt yourself in the process. Here's an example based on my experience with a client who was a man of extremely few words. He was the only guy I knew who had the unique talent of being able to answer almost any open-ended question with just one or two words.

During our consultation, I asked him how he would handle the following question: "What have you been doing with yourself since your last job?" His answer was a perfect example of how he could answer an open-ended question with only one word. He said, "Nothing."

Now to him, that was an honest answer. However, I started to ask him for some specifics on what he was doing and learned that he was reading the newspaper more regularly as well as a couple of books a month, fixing friends' cars for a bit of money, spending more time with his family, and conducting a job search.

While "nothing" was an honest answer, wouldn't it have been equally honest to expand just a little and share all that other stuff? If you were to read the second half of that last paragraph out loud, and time yourself as you did, you'd discover that it takes less than 15 seconds to answer the question with those activities.

Yet that focused, short answer would send out several subconscious messages to the interviewer. The interviewer would hear:

- That my client is not lazy.
- That he's interested in learning, staying on top of current events, and that he's literate.
- That he's staying current with his mechanical skills.
- That he's recognized in his circle of friends as an expert mechanic.
- That he has family values. He makes sure to provide an income, even when between jobs, and to spend time with his family.
- He's actively pursuing employment.

Now the fact is that this particular client was not a mechanic. He was a hydraulics man. But these two fields are loosely related (second cousins, maybe?) and they both require a mechanical mind. So remember, just because you are not doing something specifically in your field does not mean that it can't be used to your advantage. And even if it is in a totally different field, remember those transferable skills and be sure to mention them.

Another point on honesty is that you can and should be selective on which examples you use when answering interviewers' questions. For example, if they ask you to explain a time when you had a disagreement with management, you don't have to share the worst disagreement, or one that ended in a bad way. Think before you answer and give them an honest answer that won't be able to be used against you. Furthermore, if they ask for an example, don't feel obligated to share every example. If they ask for one, share one, and one only.

Another fundamental, which relates nicely to that last point, is to be focused in your answers. When employers ask questions, they want the answer to their question, and usually only the answer to their question. If you babble on and on, they are not impressed.

This is a good time to share an interviewer's secret. Interviewers will sometimes ask questions specifically to see how focused you are. For example, "Tell me about yourself" really is a bad interview question. However, it is one that is usually asked. Why? Because interviewers want to know if you are focused. If you are, you won't answer the question immediately. Instead, you'll ask something like, "Where would you like me to begin?" or "What would you like to know?" (Tricky, huh?)

Another little secret is that if interviewers want more information, they'll simply keep quiet after you finish your answer. Before long the silence will get to you and you'll start talking a bit more. The way to deal with this is that after answering the question, stay quiet. Practice a little reverse psychology on the interviewer and before long the silence will get to him and he'll ask another question.

If you can't stand the silence, another thing to do is to simply ask the interviewer if he would like to know more. Yet a third method is to politely inform him that you have finished your answer and are ready for the next question.

Some types of work are specific to a particular industry, and others are practiced in all industries. The field of accounting, for example, is done in all industries.

If your type of work is like this, and you find yourself interviewing for a position that is in an industry that you are not familiar with, be sure to get familiar with it before your interview. One client did this very well before flying more than 2,000 miles for an interview. Her experience up to that point had been in manufacturing and government, yet the position she was interviewing for was with a hospital.

Realizing that she knew next to nothing about the hospital industry, she contacted a friend who was a nurse at a local hospital. He agreed to meet with her to talk about his industry for an hour–in other words, to network with her. While they met, he showed her the services that the hospital offered. He also was able to tell her some current issues that would probably be "hot" for them, and he reviewed with her what each of those services consisted of.

Now she knew full well that she was not interviewing for a medical position. However, she knew that medically minded people would be interviewing her, and she wanted to be able to understand any issues they might share with her during the interview. By meeting with her nurse friend before taking off on that trip, she was at least familiar with some basic issues and terms.

When interviewing, you should almost always answer the question that is asked. I mention this because I can't begin to tell you the number of times that I've asked an interviewee one thing, and he's given me a completely unrelated answer.

For example, if you are asked to tell about your experience doing a particular job at employer "X," don't go into a narrative about your experience doing that same job at employer "Y." If you do this, the employer is likely to think that you are trying to hide something. It is acceptable to briefly mention that you gained further experience doing that job at the other employer, but you shouldn't go into it unless asked to do so.

There are times, however, when it is acceptable to answer with something other than what was asked. Knowing when to do this has to do with knowing what interviewers are after when they ask certain questions. A lot of times, this is the case when they ask questions that could be considered illegal.

For example, an interviewer might ask how many children you have, or how old you are. Both of these are generally considered to be illegal questions. And the interviewer probably isn't really too concerned with the number of children or your age.

With the question about children, what the interviewer probably wants to know is if you're going to be able to make it to work on time or if you'll have to take a lot of time off when your children get sick. With the age question, the interviewer probably is concerned with whether you're healthy enough for the job or whether you're planning on retiring in three or four months.

So if you're asked one of these possibly illegal questions, you could answer the unasked concern instead. For example, when you're asked about the number of children, say something like, "Well, yes I do have children; however, they are wonderful little tykes and I certainly don't see any problems with being able to get to work on time or having to take time off work to care for them."

Sometimes, however, "illegal" questions are asked with no hidden agendas at all. They might be part of the small talk before or after the interview, and can be a great way of building the rapport that you need so badly. Whether you answer the question straight out or follow the suggestions in the preceding paragraphs is up to you. Determining factors should be your comfort level and how you read the situation. And remember—a question just might be more job-related than you know, so an open mind is generally best.

In truth, there really is no such thing as an illegal interview question. In other words, there is no law that contains a list of forbidden interview questions.

However, employers are supposed to only ask about BFOQs (Bona Fide Occupational Qualifications). Their questions are supposed to be non-discriminatory and job-related. But, because there are so many thousands of different jobs in this country, our lawmakers can't come up with a specific list of outlawed questions.

For example, while a manufacturer probably shouldn't ask about the number of children you have, a school district or day care probably could.

Having children might be able to be a BFOQ for positions with the school and day care.

Some questions are asked so the interviewer can find out something else about you. For example, if an interviewer asks about your favorite sport, she rarely cares what that sport is. What she wants to know is whether you are a team player.

What you need to think about is the job you are applying for. If it is a job where you'll be alone a lot, then you might want to share one of your favorite "loner" sports. If the job requires teamwork, then pick one that tells that story.

Another question that is often asked is, "What are your weaknesses?" When employers ask this, they don't expect you to go on for half an hour about all of your personal shortcomings. However, saying that you haven't got any isn't the best answer either. The best bet is to simply pick one or two, and in the same breath that you mention them, mention how you have been improving in those areas, or what you have been proactively doing to prevent them from continuing to be weaknesses. When sharing mistakes that you've made, it's always good to show how you learned from them.

And, of course, if you can pick a weakness that could also be considered a strength, that's always a good idea, too. For example, being a perfection-ist is a weakness that could be viewed by an employer as a strength. Another might be that co-workers sometimes think that you are a bit unsociable because you don't hang out in the break room as much as they'd like you to.

When asked about your strengths, you'll want to be able to back your answers with concrete examples. Being able to define results with actual numbers will do wonders for demonstrating that you really have done what you say you have, and it shows scope.

Since specialization isn't as sought after as it once was, you won't want to define your scope too narrowly–instead, show that you are (or can be) adaptable to a changing work environment. At the same time, however, you won't want to indicate that you can do anything and everything under the sun. Such an answer doesn't show focus.

One frequently asked question that can cause anxiety for some interviewees is, "Why are you on the job market?" In today's world, having been laid off is no longer considered a terribly bad thing, and job-hopping also is tolerated much more. If, however, you were fired, or have just been released from prison, or have some other negative reason for looking for a job, then here are a few tips for you.

Answer the question directly, briefly, and honestly. A simple, straightforward answer is best. And, be sure to answer quickly and without breaking eye contact. This is probably the one question, more than any other, where interviewers are specifically looking for signs of deception.

Depending upon the position you are applying for, and the skill of the interviewer, some questions you are asked might be attempts to test your integrity. Here's an example. "Have you ever stolen a pen, pencil, paper clip, or other office materials from an employer?"

Since nearly everyone has walked out of the office with a company pen in his pocket at least once, it would probably raise doubts about your honesty if you were to say that you hadn't. However, to simply say yes wouldn't do you justice either. A good response would be something like, "Well, I have inadvertently left at the end of a day with a pen in my pocket. However, I certainly don't make a habit of it, and have returned the item when it came to my attention."

Another way interviewers test your integrity, as well as your consistency, is to have different interviewers ask you the same question during different interviews. Comparing notes later, they'll be able to check you out against yourself.

What about how to answer all those other questions? The best thing to do is to develop answers to questions before you get to the interview. To do this, go to the appendix called "101 Sample Interview Questions" at the back of this book and work on the questions listed. As you develop answers, practice saying them out loud to someone you know (someone in your network would be ideal), or with your professional career coach.

Another thing you should do is develop answers to questions that your particular background will beg answers to. For example, when my client switched from coal mining to purchasing, you can bet that he was asked about why he was making that switch.

When developing answers in advance, do not let the answers come out as though they have been prepared in advance. This will cause the interviewer to think that the information you are sharing isn't as "pure" as it could be. So, if the interviewer asks a question that you already know the answer to, go ahead and let it look like you're thinking of an answer before blurting it out. Become a bit of an actor or actress and remember that timing can count as much as anything else. Your answers will sound more natural this way, and it communicates to the interviewer that you like to think before responding to questions. Remember, recruitment is a game–play the game.

Once you feel fairly confident about how to answer interview questions, participate in some mock interviews. This is where you get somebody, who knows how to do it, to actually interview you. Have this person review your resume, and maybe even an application that you've filled out, and then ask you whatever questions he would normally ask.

The real advantage to mock interviews is in having the interviewer critique you immediately after the interview. Unlike employers, who are rarely willing to go out on a limb and tell you what you did right and wrong, someone doing a mock interview will. And, of course, if you videotape it, you'll be able to rewind and actually see any areas for improvement. While watching such a video, constantly be asking yourself, "Would I hire this person?"

The key on mock interviews is to have someone do it that normally does interviews. For this reason, H.R. professionals are generally the best because it's their job to interview, and you can bet that they do it more than anyone else in their company. This is one reason it's a good idea to have at least one H.R. professional in your network. Experienced hiring authorities are available to do this for you through The Job Search Advisor, Incorporated. To find one in your area go to ***www.jobsearchadvisor.com.***

Immediately after any real interview (though it wouldn't be a bad idea to do after mock interviews, too), be sure to take detailed notes. You'll want to record who interviewed you (with a correctly spelled name and title), where the interview took place (his office only? or did it include a tour?), when it happened (date, time, how long, etc.), and what was discussed (questions asked, answers, general discussion, etc.). You should do this for each person you spoke with.

Your notes should include everything that you can remember, including any personal information about the interviewer. This way, if the interviewer mentioned that his daughter was sick, you'll be sure to ask about her next time you get to talk with that person. These notes will also help you "tweak" your job search efforts.

When interviewing for a position, take advantage of any opportunity that you can to get in front of the employer, even if you have to create such opportunities yourself. This will help to refresh the employer's memory of you. Since most candidates don't do this, you will be the person that pops to mind whenever the employer thinks about the position. What's more, it'll further demonstrate that you really want that job.

One of my favorite examples of this happened with a client named Von. After all the interviews had been completed, the company was planning to take about a week to make a decision. During this week, Von was to have his alma mater send the company a copy of his university transcripts.

Rather than passively waiting around hoping and praying, Von decided to make one more interview opportunity for himself. Toward the end of the week he got dressed up in his best interview suit and drove to his university to get his transcripts. He then drove over to the employer and walked on over to the reception area outside of the hiring manager's office.

The receptionist recognized him, since he had made a point to be extremely friendly each time he had come in to interview, and asked if she could help him. He said that she could in just a bit, but first he wanted to look at some of the plaques on the wall.

While loitering there, Von made pleasant small talk with the receptionist and others who came in, and after about 10 minutes, the manager came through on her way to her office. Seeing Von, she gave him a happy smile of recognition and asked what he was doing.

He said that he "happened to be in the neighborhood," so thought he'd stop in to drop his transcripts off. His response very much reminded me of a line in the movie *Arthur*. At one point, Linda had crashed Arthur's engagement party and when he asked her what she was doing there, she replied with something like, "I was in the neighborhood; it took me two buses, three cabs, and a train to get in the neighborhood but what the [heck]."

Some people would say that Von was lucky that the hiring manager happened to walk by and maybe he was. But I'll tell you this, if he hadn't dressed up and taken the time to go there, he wouldn't have been so "lucky." In other words, in your job search you can significantly increase your chances of being lucky through preparation, creativity, and going the extra mile!

By the way, after Von answered her question, she invited him to her office and, thanks to the rapport he had built during previous meetings, they chatted like old friends. Half an hour later he was on his way, and about two days after that she called with the job offer!

Chapter Eighteen

References

Smart employers check references. There are several different types of references, and it is your responsibility to know which ones are available to you as well as which ones "sell" you the best for each position you are attempting to secure.

One type of reference is the letter of recommendation. It is great if you can get these from employers; however, you do not want to include a bunch of these with your resume when you initially turn it in. The same can be said of performance evaluations, school transcripts, certificates from seminars, and other such documents.

Of course, every rule has its exceptions. One exception would be if an employer asks for such documentation to accompany your original application materials. Another exception is that some employers, for some types of positions, actually do want volumes of information with the initial application. When this is desired, the employer will typically ask for a curriculum vita. This is appropriate for certain positions in academia, research, government, the medical field, and for some engineering positions.

Other than the exceptions mentioned, few employers appreciate it when they get 10, 20, 30, or more pages with an initial application. During the initial stages of the screening process, most employers simply don't have time, nor do they care, to review such documentation. Including one or possibly even two letters of recommendation can be acceptable if they say things that are specific to the particular job for which you are applying.

For example, if you are applying for a position as an administrative assistant, and you have a one-page letter of recommendation from a recognized employer in the area, and if that letter specifically speaks to your knowledge, skills, and abilities as an administrative assistant, then it could be acceptable to include the one letter along with your original application materials.

If, however, that letter only talks about what a great person you are, and does not speak to the specific knowledge, skills, and abilities that the employer you are applying at is looking for, then don't include it with your original application materials.

If you have three, 10, or 20 such letters, then you'll want to pick out the one or two that sell you the best. This same example can be used for performance evaluations, certificates of seminar attendance, awards and honors, and so forth.

If you do decide to include any of this type of documentation with your original application, then you should highlight the specific words that do you the most good. This way, the employer won't have to read the entire letter. Remember, you want to make it as easy as possible for the employer's decision-makers.

You'll notice that throughout this discussion I have indicated that you don't want to include this documentation with the original application materials. It is certainly advisable, however, to bring copies along with you to any interview. This way, you can mention you have them and if the interviewers look interested, you can show them. Forcing them to review the information will only cause them to resent you, and will do nothing to win them to your side. For more on this, see the chapter called "Your Portfolio."

Why wouldn't interviewers want to see such information? There are several reasons. One might be for consistency. If they don't request this type of information from all applicants, then it may be legally advisable for them to not accept it from any candidates. Another reason is that they simply might not have time to review it. A third reason is that for a lot of employers, an official reference check (conducted by their own staffs) is more preferred than a written letter of recommendation.

Now that we've talked a bit about written references, let's talk about the verbal ones. Before we get into the meat of this subject, let's cover two basics. First, always get someone's permission before putting him down as a reference. Second, make absolutely certain that the phone number you list is a current one and includes an area code.

When I speak of references, I am not necessarily speaking about the name of your most recent supervisor that you put down on your application. The reason for this is that the application typically asks for your most recent supervisor, and this may or may not be the best person to include on your list of references.

For example, what if you worked for 10 years for one supervisor and then one month before leaving your last employer, you got a new one? When the application asks for the name and phone number of your most recent supervisor, it would be inaccurate to say that it was the one you'd had for 10 years.

If space permits, you should put both of them—even if the one you had for 10 years is no longer with that employer. If space does not permit, then on the application put the one that is asked for, and on your list of references put the other. Of course, you should only include the supervisor you had for 10 years if he would say good things about you.

On your list of references, be sure to include your references' names, titles, addresses, phone numbers, e-mail addresses, and how they knew you. The statement of how they knew you should be short, such as, "My direct supervisor at XYZ Company for 10 years," or "Co-worker at Widget Inc. for the last 4 years."

If you're applying for a different kind of work than what your experience speaks to, and if you must put a reference from that experience, be sure to coach the person you are using as your reference to be sure that she emphasizes your transferable skills and not the actual job itself.

It is advisable to have a good idea of what your references are going to say. If they are personal friends, or if you have established a really good professional relationship with them, this will be easy. If, however, they do not fit into one of these categories, then you should ask someone to call them and do a reference check on you. This way, you'll know what they are telling employers about you.

For obvious reasons you couldn't do this yourself because the information shared wouldn't be the same as when someone else does it. There is a sample reference check form in the appendix of this book.

When you do this, be sure that the person conducting the reference checks for you not only listens to the specific words they use, but also to the attitude they share. For example, a previous supervisor might use words that indicate he can't share information, yet how he says this could communicate volumes about whether he'd recommend you for anything.

If you learn that a former employer is giving out information that could be detrimental to your ability to acquire future employment, there are several things you might be able to do. First of all, if the employer has a policy of not giving out such information, then a simple phone call to the H.R. or Legal department should put an end to it. This will be especially true if you are clear about sharing the time and date of the reference check, actual quotes, and other specifics.

If a previous supervisor is giving out a negative reference, and the employer doesn't have a policy against it, then there are at least three things you could do. Naturally, the first would be to simply ask the person not to share such information. Quite often there are bad feelings after an employee leaves and letting a little time pass, followed by a simple, polite, up-beat conversation with the person, can do wonders for mending relationships.

Another thing you could do is confront the person or his Legal or H.R. department and let them know that you know what they are saying about you. Oftentimes, knowing that you know will make them self-conscious and result in their not doing it anymore.

If this doesn't work, you could tell them that you feel this information is erroneous and not truly representative of your actual contribution at that employer, and that you may find it necessary to hold them legally liable for any damages this information ends up causing you. Upon learning that you know what they are saying about you, and that you may decide to pursue legal action if it persists, they are very likely to put a stop to it.

Yet another thing to do is to be sure to be honest with anyone that you interview with. If there's a chance that a previous employer will be sharing negative information about your employment situation, cover it in the interview so the potential employer hears it from you and not from your previous employer.

One time I was following up with a client who had been fired from his previous employer for not following company policy. He ended up getting a much better position with a much better employer, partially due to how he handled the "having been fired" issue.

During the interview he had been totally honest and had shared that he had been fired for not following a company policy. By way of explanation, he let them know that while it was a policy that everybody broke, the fact of the matter was that it was a policy, and he knew it, and he had broken it. In other words, he took responsibility for having broken it. And he didn't go on for 20 minutes about his negative feelings toward that previous employer. He covered it and then allowed the interview to continue.

When it got to the point of the interviewer asking for my client's references, he was able to remind the interviewer that he'd been fired, and thus probably wouldn't get a very good reference. The interviewer replied, "Well, you were honest with me, so let me be honest with you. All we do is verify dates of employment, so you'll be fine."

There are two final H.R. secrets I'd like to share with you about how some companies do reference checks. The first has to do with the fact that most companies are smart enough to realize that you handpick whoever you have on your list of references. So, naturally, their references would give nothing but glowing recommendations. Therefore, some companies will ask certain questions during the interview specifically to get names of other individuals who might be able to provide a more well-rounded picture of what you have to offer.

For example, they might ask you to share a time when you had a major disagreement with a manager and how you worked it out. You might start off by saying, "Well there was this one manager who…" to which they might interrupt and ask for the manager's name. If they do this, then more than likely they are making note of that manager's name so they can follow up with her and get her side of the story.

How do you handle such a situation? When the interviewers ask questions, make sure to only give answers that will result in helping you get the position. In the above example, when they ask you to share that "major disagreement with a manager," don't just give them the first one that comes to your mind. Instead, think of a situation where the disagreement really worked out to everyone's satisfaction and where the manager ended up being someone who thought highly of you. This way, if they end up contacting the manager, they'll get the same story that you told, and a good recommendation to boot!

The final secret you should be aware of is that interviewers will sometimes ask a certain question, phrased a particular way, specifically because they don't plan on actually contacting the reference. While this isn't always the case, more than one employer has told me that they do this. The question is, "What will your former manager tell us about you when we contact her?" The idea behind asking in this way is that the applicant will be inclined to answer more honestly than he might otherwise because the interviewer has indicated that he will contact the reference to verify what the applicant has said. Employers have shared with me that they do this because it can be a great way to find out what a reference would probably say without having to actually contact her.

Before leaving this subject, there are still a few procedural things you should be aware of. The first is that references can take a very long time to obtain–sometimes several weeks! There are many reasons that it can take so long, such as the workload of staff conducting reference checks; not having a good address or phone number for references; references being unavailable due to a business trip, vacation, or sick leave; references not returning phone calls; and having to play "phone tag" for days on end.

And, even if your references come in quickly and look great, if you are one of several candidates being considered for the position, you might still have to wait for the references to come in on the other candidates.

The other procedural thing for you to know is that some employers require that reference checks be completed prior to a job offer being made. This requirement is sometimes quantified with a number and quality, such as "two good references." This can be frustrating when a supervisor has (unwisely) said you have the job, yet it's weeks before the company actually makes an official offer.

The combination of a reference check being required, yet sometimes taking a long time to complete, can be extremely frustrating to employment candidates. This is especially so when you consider that employers typically (and wisely) don't share with applicants where they are in the interview process.

There are several reasons employers don't share this information. The reason having to do with references is twofold. First, if candidates know where they are in the process, then if and when they get cut, they'll know who was responsible.

Secondly, a lot of those employment candidates would then use that knowledge in such a way as to reduce the employer's ability to obtain reference information on other applicants in the future. For example, if a candidate found out he was cut due to a bad reference, he might cause problems for the reference. This could then cause that reference to be hesitant about giving the employer a candid reference on another applicant in the future. In other words, employers want to protect the people that give them references so that they'll continue to do so.

Chapter Nineteen

Salary Negotiation

Job searches can sometimes go on for many months, a year, or even longer. When this happens, the financial situation of many job seekers becomes such that they are required to take odd jobs to make ends meet. They usually don't necessarily enjoy these jobs, and are most eager to secure a real position in their field.

This eagerness, however, should not cloud your mind of sound judgment. Toward the end of such a job search, a client of mine was selected for a fantastic position. The offer was more than what he had been making in his previous position, had better benefits, and was in a great environment.

As desperate as he was for a career position in his field, he did not immediately accept the position. Instead, he worded (and timed) his response as I had taught him to do, and within about 30 seconds, the offer was raised by several thousand dollars. Did you catch that? In half a minute, he made several thousand dollars! And that was a public sector job, where some people believe negotiation is not even possible!

Before we get into actual negotiation techniques and tactics, let's discuss the employer's frame of mind when he makes the job offer. The most important thing to know is that when an employer makes a job offer, the roles have changed. The dynamics of your relationship with the employer are completely different.

Prior to the job offer, you were selling and the employer was buying. Once the offer is made, the employer is selling and you are buying. This is an extremely important concept to understand in order to negotiate the best deal.

The reason for this role reversal is that prior to the offer, the employer had several (maybe even several hundred) candidates from which to choose. By making you the offer, the employer is letting you know that you are the one he wants. Once that decision has been made, the employer doesn't want to lose you. This is the reason that it's only after the offer that you are in a position to ask for more money, benefits, perks, etc.

Another thing to know about the employer's frame of mind is that when recruiting for a position, it is usually several weeks and sometimes several months before the employer actually gets to the point of being able to make an offer. During this time, business typically suffers because no one is in the position. Therefore, when the recruiter finally gets around to making an offer, he is generally as eager about having you accept it as you were that you'd get the offer.

As far as negotiating your salary, the first rule is that you never mention compensation until after the employer does. There are many reasons for this, but for the purposes of this discussion I'll share only one: to bring it up first could cause the employer to think that you are only interested in the position for the money. Hopefully, this is not the case. Employers want people who are looking for an overall fit within a company and not just a financial fit.

This does not mean, however, that you should go into an initial inter-view, and subsequently go completely through the interview process, without having any idea of what the position pays. Doing a little research through the Internet or through your network should provide you with a ballpark figure of what the position should pay so that you'll know whether to spend time pursuing it.

The second rule is that you never discuss actual numbers until an offer has been made. Remember, until that point, the company is merely shop-ping around. Once the company decides it wants you, then the bargaining can begin. If the recruiter wants to discuss compensation before making the offer, try one of the following suggestions.

One option is to skirt the question with a statement about how the overall fit is more important at this stage and that you'd be willing to discuss compensation after learning more about the position. A second option is to state that you simply expect a fair salary based upon your skills and abilities. A third option is to indicate that you'd prefer to discuss it only after an offer has been made. A final suggestion, if you want to try a little humor, could be to say that you expect to get paid as much as they can afford and not a penny less!

Prior to an offer, employers want to discuss compensation for one of two reasons: to screen people out or to save money. If the recruiter asks what it would take for you to accept an offer, and you mention a salary that is too high, the recruiter will simply screen you out and you'll be out of the running. If you mention a salary that is too low, the recruiter might screen you out figuring that you must not be worth what he thought you were worth. Or, he might go ahead and hire you at the figure you mentioned even though the company might have been willing to pay much more. If you mention just the right number, all might be OK but you'll always wonder if you could have negotiated for more. The black and white of the matter is that it is never in the applicant's best interest to discuss money before the employer has made an offer.

When you get to the point of being offered a position, here's a rule that you should always follow: Repeat the figure offered, or the top of the range mentioned, and then look down at your feet for about 30 seconds (do not look at your watch or at a clock in the room). It's important that you repeat the figure or top of the range mentioned so that the recruiter doesn't think that you didn't hear him.

Since the roles were just reversed and the recruiter is now "selling," his anxiety will rise as the seconds tick by. While you are silently waiting for the 30 seconds to pass, the recruiter will wonder if the offer was too low. Oftentimes the recruiter will interrupt the silence with a better offer.

If this happens, simply repeat the higher number and then look down at your feet for another 30 seconds. Once the time has passed, look up and respond honestly. At this point a discussion concerning the dollar amount would be appropriate. If the offer is too low, try reminding the recruiter of the knowledge, skills, and abilities that you will bring to the company.

Once a dollar figure has been established, accept the figure, but not the position. Many applicants forget about benefits, perks, future raises, and other items that could significantly increase the overall compensation package. Be sure that you don't accept the position until you have the package that suits you. If this means having to think about it for a few days, then so be it. Most employers see nothing wrong with an applicant taking some time to think about an offer or to discuss it with his or her spouse. You will never have a better time to negotiate such things, as you will before you accept the position.

Most job seekers simply accept the first offer that's made, when it's made, and feel that they've been successful. Of course in hourly or entry-level jobs this might be the case. However, a lot of offers have some room for negotiation, and if you don't try, you'll never know.

In my professional experience, I've nearly always had more money I could offer applicants for salaried positions. Sadly, however, about eight out of 10 accept the first figure mentioned and we end the negotiations before they ever begin. I've always felt bad for them when all they would have had to do was ask and they'd have gotten a better offer.

People who negotiate a better compensation package win in several ways. The obvious way is that they get more in their paycheck from day one. Another way is that by successfully negotiating a better compensation package they are reaffirming in the employer's mind that they really were the best choice. A third way they win is that all future raises are based upon current earnings. For example, 5 percent of $65,000 is more than 5 percent of $60,000.

Of course, one big reason that applicants accept the first offer that comes along is because all they can think about is getting the job.

Oftentimes they've spent hundreds of dollars, as well as hundreds of hours, conducting a job search and by the time they get an offer they don't want to risk losing it. After having spent hours, days, weeks, and even months trying to get the job, they wrap it up in less than two seconds.

What you have to keep in mind is the thought mentioned earlier. Throughout your job search you were selling, but now that an offer has been made the dynamics have changed. Play your cards right and you will see the money–and benefits to boot!

If you get an offer from one employer and sense that you're about to get another offer from a different employer, then it's perfectly acceptable to refrain from making a decision on the first one until you know about the second. As mentioned, most employers don't object to giving you a few days to make a decision. You should not, however, keep them waiting too long.

Another thing you should not do is try to play one employer against the other. Sure, it's possible that one employer might raise its offer in an attempt to get you to accept the position. However, it's also very possible that the employer will figure that you're only after the money. People who are only interested in the money tend to job hop every time a better deal comes along, and most employers don't want to be bothered with such people.

There is one book that I recommend more than any other on this subject. It's called *Salary Negotiation–How to make $1,000 a minute.* It is by Jack Chapman and was first published in 1987 by Ten Speed Press, which operates out of Berkeley, California.

You can see why I did not recommend this book in the very first paragraph of this chapter. When I recommend it to people (which I always do during any discussion or seminar on this topic), they generally think that it's some sort of hoax or bait. They simply can't believe that it can be possible. It is possible, and if you'd like to learn how to do it, you owe it to yourself to get the book.

I recommend his book due to my experience on both sides of the desk. As an employer I can confirm that he knows well what goes on in the mind of employers during salary negotiation. As a job seeker, since first reading his book I have personally applied his techniques and have successfully negotiated every job offer prior to acceptance by several thousand dollars!

I do not get any royalties from any sales of his book, and I don't know the author. I do know, however, that his advice works.

Chapter Twenty

The Internet

The Internet has completely changed many aspects of how job seekers conduct their job search. Every week there is new technology with new implications for job seekers. The following information is meant as an overview of some of the things you should be aware of as you think to use the Internet in your job search.

For starters, using the Internet in your job search can become very time-consuming. For many of us it would be easy to end up spending hundreds of hours a month surfing the Net in the name of our job search. Before you fall into this trap, keep in mind the type and extent of your job search. If you are only looking locally, then your use of the Internet would be significantly different than if you are looking globally. Other factors that are influential as you are determining how much to use the Internet include your comfort level with computers, the level of the position you are seeking, and how much time you have to invest in your job search.

The Internet is fantastic at helping job seekers with employer and industry research. Many employers have an "employment opportunities" page that lists their current openings and information on how to apply. Many of these sites allow you to apply on-line. These sites also provide a lot of other valuable information about the employer, such as their products, history, mission, etc.

You can also use the Internet to do some job search research. For example, there are some excellent sites comparing the cost of living between various cities. Another way to use the Internet is to do some very basic salary research. However, when doing either of these types of research, be extremely careful of the validity of the information. For example, many cost of living sites are based solely on real estate and most salary comparison sites are self-reported. Neither of these data sources is to be considered valid.

Job search research on the Internet can also include visiting any of the thousands of sites dedicated to helping job seekers. A better use of your time, however, would be to hire a Job Search Advisor for an hour or two who knows the best information and would share the relevant knowledge with you, as well as how to apply it to your particular situation. To find a Job Search Advisor in your area, go to *www.jobsearchadvisor.com.*

Many job boards allow you to post your resume. This is something you should do. "Search Agents" are another significant tool. Unbelievably, this is one of those few things in life that is of incredible value, yet is free! A search agent is like a mini-Web-crawler who goes out every day and searches for newly posted positions that meet your criteria. Basically, it does much of your Internet job search for you. It then e-mails you, usually daily, letting you know of the positions and where to go to find them. Now if that isn't cool, I don't know what is!

Chapter Twenty-one

Career Fairs

When attending Career Fairs, most job seekers seem to fit into one of three categories. The first category is individuals who come unprepared and simply wander aimlessly around. These people conduct an ineffective job search. The second type of job seeker shoots from one employer booth to the next. She generally appears too intent on "the mission," and comes across to the employer-representatives as a wound-up robot. The third type comes to see one or two specific employers. This individual arrives, does his thing, and then leaves. The third type, with some tweaking, might be acceptable to employers if he is currently employed and is only interested in employment with those specific employers. However, if you are conducting a complete job search, none of these three types is the way to approach a career fair.

The first thing you should do to prepare for a career fair is schedule at least one full day. If it is a multiple-day event, plan to attend for more than one day if your schedule permits and if a sufficient number of employers are participating.

Next, you will want to do research on the participating employers. To do this, contact the sponsoring organization for a list of participants. Once you have the list, contact the companies and ask about their current openings and the names/titles of their hiring managers. It would be best if you could also obtain copies of actual job descriptions. Otherwise, obtain brief summaries of the responsibilities and qualifications for the positions that interest you. Once you are aware of which companies are recruiting for the type of career expertise that you offer, you will be ready to begin the employer research. Please see the Job Search Research chapter for this critical piece of preparation for a career fair.

Next you will want to prepare customized resumes for the particular employers and positions that interest you. This can be as simple as changing the objective on a generic resume, or as involved as a complete rewrite. When writing such a resume, remember to use the key words that you know are important to the employer (based on your research).

There will probably be hundreds of job seekers competing with you at the career fair. Every one of them will have brought resumes to hand out to the employers at the career fair. Only a few, however, will have brought cover letters too. And fewer still will have the employer representatives' name on the cover letter. If you really want to stand out, you need to be diligent about obtaining this information and use it to your advantage.

You should also bring several generic resumes. Depending upon your particular background and the manner in which your field can be divided, they could all be the same generic resume or you could bring several copies each of different generic resumes. For example, in my field of Human Resources, I could have one generic resume showing that I am a generalist with experience in all areas of the field. I could also have a separate generic resume for each specialization found in HR–a generic recruiting resume, a generic training resume, a generic benefits administration resume, and so on.

Prior to showing up at the career fair, develop a plan of action so as to avoid wasting time on less important activities. Naturally, you will first want to pursue the specific employers for whom you have researched and prepared customized materials. This might be a list of anywhere from about three to ten employers. While at the fair, be sure to visit the booths of these "priority employers" several times, especially when they do not have other job seekers monopolizing the representatives' time.

Your plan of action should also include a second list of employers of possible interest. These will be the employers to whom you would probably hand your generic resumes and with whom you would spend time between visits to the "priority employers." In other words, you might try to get around to all the priority employers first, then spend an hour "working" the second list of employers, followed by revisiting the priority employers, and so on.

Another part of your plan of action concerns any seminars or other activities that might be available. You should review the fair schedule and plan to attend as many as might be of benefit to you.

After the career fair, follow-up is absolutely essential. Remember, the employer representatives who attended the fair will be getting back to their offices with hundreds of resumes, several days of work that they will now be behind on, and the pressing need to fill the openings that they had gone to the fair to fill. Proper follow-up can help them to remember you and could help you become the applicant of choice!

The first follow-up activity you should do is to send each employer representative with whom you spoke a personalized thank you letter. Be sure to include a copy of your resume with this letter. If you spoke with three different people from the same company, you should send three separate letters—one to each of them. If the employer representative mentioned a manager's name that they thought you should contact, it would be wise to send that individual a letter too.

While visiting with the employer representatives at the career fair, you should have asked them about their time line on filling the position and if they had any advice on how you should follow up. Naturally, you will generally want to operate within any such time lines and advice. However, depending upon the company, their recruitment needs, the individual with whom you happened to speak, or any number of other reasons, it may also be wise to touch base with them prior to what they had suggested. One thing to keep in mind, however, is that at this point in the game you don't want to get on anyone's bad side.

Finally, it is essential that you use your time wisely while waiting for their next move. The way to do this is to do some further research on the companies so you'll be prepared for an interview should one be offered. When following up, it is certainly appropriate to ask about the status of the recruitment campaign. When doing this, be prepared to ask a few questions so they can see how interested and intelligent you are. And remember, employers generally hire whom they like, so be sure to be likable too!

Chapter Twenty-two

Following Up and Thank You Letters

Following up is yet another absolutely essential and strategic aspect of your job search, especially with your network and interview contacts. It is also an area that most applicants mess up fairly regularly, which means that doing a good job here could help make you look great in comparison to other applicants. Whether following up with network contacts or interviewers, the rules are about the same.

In following up, you most definitely do not want to become a hassle or bother to someone. On the other hand, you don't want the person to forget you either. It is vital that you strike a balance somewhere between these two extremes.

The best way to not become a hassle or bother is to be sensitive to the other person's situation and to be respectful. This seems to be difficult for most applicants because they need a job. Their thoughts are all self-centered, which leaves them little chance of being sensitive and respectful of the other person.

Take the case of Dale. He was an employment candidate who had impressed one of my employer friends, and my friend really did want to see him hired. However, the position he interviewed for ended up being put on hold. He wisely asked if he could follow up, and my friend gladly said that he could.

Variables that were out of my friend's control affected the position, and while the position wasn't canceled, the company wasn't pursuing it either.

Eventually, my friend had to inform Dale that he really didn't have any idea of when they'd be able to move ahead with this position, and let him know that he'd call him as soon as he heard differently.

In the weeks and months that followed, Dale began to call my friend two and three times a week. It got to the point that my friend dreaded the sound of his voice on the phone. Initially, my friend had been very much in Dale's court; however, as he took more and more of Dale's calls, he lost all desire to ever hear from or see him again.

Dale might have thought that my friend was "blowing him off" when he initially said he'd call him when the company began to move on the position again. In fact, my friend was not blowing him off, and if he had only contacted my friend every two or three weeks, Dale wouldn't have lost his vote. In situations like this, it really is best to take whatever the company representative tells you at face value, and do what you can to maintain the relationship. To do more could ruin it!

Whether dealing with a network contact or an interviewer, you'll want to ask if it's OK to follow up, and if so, how often and in what manner. Unless the person suggests something else, I'd recommend that you alternate between phone calls and letters. Do one or the other about every two or three weeks. Had Dale done this, then my friend would have only heard his voice on the phone about every month to a month and a half, and he would have remained in my friend's favor.

Depending upon the situation, and your relationship with the person, some of the phone calls could be nothing more than voice messages simply letting the individual know that you are still alive and seeking employment. Such messages could indicate that a return call isn't necessary, thereby showing the person that you respect his valuable time, although you should still leave your number just in case he wants to get in touch with you.

Thank you letters are a type of follow-up communication. After any interview, always send thank you letters. Make absolutely certain that names and titles are correct and spelled correctly. These should be sharp-looking, short, to the point, and refer to something specific that was discussed in the interview. Of course, the same is generally done after any networking meeting, too.

If you interviewed with eight different people, then you should send eight different thank you letters. They will probably all end up in the same file, so this would allow you eight different opportunities to show off what you have to offer. Furthermore, with today's customer service mentality, employers will appreciate that you're the type of person to personalize each letter, as opposed to merely changing the inside address on your computer eight different times.

Should you type or hand-write the letter? There are different schools of thought on this. A compromise might be to type it and then hand-write a short, personal note at the bottom. Writing the whole thing by hand is acceptable if you have neat handwriting.

Timing-wise, you should mail your letter so that it is received at the beginning of a new week. Mail that comes in at the end of the week is soon forgotten. The exception to this would be if the employer you interviewed with had indicated that a decision would be made by the end of the week. Of course, there is no way to guarantee that it would be delivered, routed, and read by any particular day, but you can make a logical guess and hope for the best.

Chapter Twenty-three

Your Portfolio

In some professions, a portfolio is as basic to the job search as a resume. Artists, photographers, and architects, for example, wouldn't dream of going to an interview without a portfolio. Inside their portfolios are samples of their best work.

Other professions do the same thing, but they might not officially call it a portfolio. Writers, for example, generally bring writing samples to an interview. While they might not call it a portfolio, it serves the same purpose. Radio disc jockeys are another example. They wouldn't dream of going to an interview without an audiotape that demonstrates how they sound on the air.

People in any profession can develop, and then use, a portfolio to their job search advantage. This is true even if it's not normally done in your particular line of work. If that describes your situation, then when you show up with a sharp and professional-looking portfolio, employers are likely to be even more impressed.

Regardless of whether they look at it, a portfolio lets them know that not only are you prepared, but that you're the type of person who goes all out doing things that no one else would bother to do. And if you'll go the extra mile during your job search, they'll figure that you'll do the same once hired.

There are two parts to a portfolio and we'll be borrowing a couple of terms from the computer industry to help explain them. The first part is what we'll call "hardware." It would include the three-ring binder, the plastic see-through page protectors, and the section dividers. The "software" is everything else–all the personal stuff that is unique to you.

You'll want to be sure that your "hardware" is extremely sharp-looking. Rather than using old school supplies that you used years ago, or leftovers that your kids are finished with, invest $10 and go to an office supply store and purchase brand-new materials. Having a portfolio won't do you much good if it falls apart in the interviewer's hands!

For the purposes of this discussion, we will assume that you will be using a three-ring binder. While that would work best for most portfolios, it is not a requirement. Artists, for example, generally do not use a three-ring binder because their work wouldn't fit in it. The point is to use whatever will work for you, but whatever you use, make absolutely sure that it shows you off in the best possible manner.

If you are going to use a three-ring binder, I would recommend a hard-covered one with inside pockets. For most positions, a black one looks the most professional. And realizing that most interviewers are on a time schedule, a thinner one is better. A half-inch or one-inch binder won't scare most people, and even a one-and-a-half inch one might be okay. But if you walk in with a three-or four-inch binder, there is very little chance that anyone will want to peek inside.

The reason for this is basic human psychology. When you tell interviewers that you want to show them something, and then heft a four-inch binder up onto the desk, they will immediately think that you want to take them through it page-by-page. Being extremely busy, as most interviewers are, they won't want to let you open it for fear they'll never get rid of you. A thinner binder isn't nearly as imposing.

To aid in its professional appearance, you will want to be sure that the guts of your portfolio fit nicely inside your binder. Getting a half-inch binder that won't close by itself due to everything that is stuffed inside defeats the purpose. In such a case, it would be better to get a one-inch binder.

You will also want to use the aforementioned plastic, see-through page protectors. These will keep your documentation clean, crisp, and professional looking for as long as you might need to use the portfolio. This also keeps you from having to punch holes into your good papers.

A third element of your "hardware" will be the dividers. These are important to keep your portfolio organized. With dividers, if you want to show someone a particular sample of your work, you can flip quickly and easily right to it rather than having to hunt for it. By seeing that your portfolio is organized, they'll get the message that you are an organized person. And this just happens to be one of the things employers want in employees!

Inside the front cover, on the pocket, you might want to attach a business card from your last (or current) employer. Inside that front pocket would be a good place for several extra original copies of your resume, your list of references, a list of your university coursework and professional seminars, etc. Basically, inside that front pocket would be a good place for extra copies of anything that you might want to give your prospective employer.

Now, before we actually get into the guts, or "software," of your portfolio, let's discuss some ways to draw the interviewer's attention to specific elements. You must remember that if an interviewer opens your portfolio and sees a whole page of text, he probably won't want to go to the effort of reading the whole thing. Rather than letting him pass it by, here are some things you can do to be sure that he sees what you want him to see. Applying these methods wisely will help the important information jump out at whoever is reviewing it.

One of the best ways is to make use of a new, yellow highlighter. When you use a highlighter, remember, "less is more." This means that if you highlight half the page, you'll lose the effectiveness of the highlighter. Yellow is the best color to use because it's a happy, positive color, and it's easy to see through. Other colors are more difficult to see through and can convey negative messages to the interviewer's subconscious.

Another method that will help to make sure you get the most out of your portfolio is to write a note or two to summarize, explain, or amplify something of particular note. In one client's portfolio, for example, one memo from his supervisor to her manager indicated that he was working about 60 hours a week. He wrote a small note, which he attached to this memo, informing whoever might look at it that he was an "exempt" employee. In other words, he wasn't getting paid anything extra for all those extra hours. He did this so that they'd be sure to get the message that he was a dedicated employee!

A third method that will highlight information as well as help make your portfolio look especially good is to put a different-colored border behind smaller pieces of documentation. For example, one of my clients' portfolios included several memos from a supervisor who put her in charge of the department whenever he was out. To truly appreciate this level of responsibility, she felt it was important that anyone reading these memos know that supervisor's title. Therefore, on the first of these, she attached one of his business cards, and to make it stand out, she put a different colored-border behind it.

To summarize the combined use of some of these methods, let me share what the first page of those memos looked like in her portfolio. Up at the top she highlighted the "From: John Smith" section. She then highlighted the three or four words that specifically put her in charge, and then at the bottom she had her supervisor's business card with a border behind it. This business card, of course, matched up with the "From: John Smith" that was highlighted above. The average person could get the message of that memo in about three seconds without having to read the whole thing.

You may have noticed that the preceding paragraph mentioned that my client's portfolio included several pages of memos. It is acceptable to have more than one page in your portfolio dedicated to the same type of thing, but only if there is a reason for it. In her case, she included three of these memos to demonstrate that she was put in charge regularly, and that it wasn't just a one-time occasion.

The same logic works for every type of documentation that you decide to include in your portfolio. For example, more than one letter of recommendation is acceptable (even recommended), but more than half a dozen would be too many. Remember, you don't have a lot of space in your little half-inch (or one-inch) portfolio, so use what you do have wisely!

For any particular type of documentation that you want more than one or two of, simply select the three to six that are the best. "The best" can be decided by any of the following: the ones most relevant to the type of position for which you are applying, any that are from a noteworthy individual or employer, the most recent ones, or the ones that make it sound like you can walk on water.

In the following paragraphs we'll review the "software" that you could put into the various sections of your portfolio. Your portfolio might only have two or three sections or it might have more than a dozen. The order you put these sections in should be actively decided by you, and not just passively happen by chance. Sections, as well as the documentation within those sections, do not have to be arranged chronologically, nor should they be put in simply by the order in which you completed the sections. The determining factor should be whatever's important to the job you're applying for.

The first thing in your portfolio should be the introduction material. It would include a clean copy of your expanded resume. Following that could be a list of university coursework and professional seminars. The next thing might be your list of references. The final thing could be a copy of your one-page resume. Each of these would be in its own plastic, see-through page protector and all of this would come before the first section of the portfolio—before the first divider.

In actual sections of your portfolio, as mentioned earlier, one section could include messages where you were put in charge of a project, a department, or anything else.

Another section could have programs from various professional associations that you have been actively involved in. Naturally, you would only include programs from meetings where you are mentioned in the program, and then you would want to be sure to highlight your name and what it was that you did.

Another section could have articles that you might have written for various employer publications or professional trade journals. In this case, you'd want to highlight your byline.

Because community involvement is important to some employers, one section could include any documentation that indicates your participation in that arena. When doing this, it is generally best to steer clear of emphasizing your involvement in particular church groups and political activities because they could offend some employers or bias them. For example, I am generally very active in various groups within my church; however, my portfolio only mentions my involvement in the Boy Scouts and the Big Brothers/Big Sisters program.

Another section could be chock-full of any professional certifications or other certificates that you may have received for various seminars and other such things you've attended. You could again use a highlighter to help focus the eye of whoever might be reviewing it.

Memos to (or about) you are a great way to have a third person tell the prospective employer about your duties or responsibilities.

If you do work that gets feedback from dozens of different people, such as an information trainer gets from people she trains, then one section could have a summary of some of those evaluations.

Of course, actual samples of your work would be most appropriate for at least one section. And it would certainly be acceptable to have several such sections if your work could be divided intelligently. An example would be a weekly report that you might be responsible for putting together and then distributing.

Letters of recommendation or appreciation and performance evaluations are other sections that you could include. On these, you should definitely use the highlighter to focus your readers' eyes on the important parts.

If your line of work lends itself to your being able to take pictures of completed projects, then one section could be full of photographs. In such cases, if there is detail work that you'd want an interviewer to see, you might want to cut an arrow out of a yellow 3x5 card and then attach it to the photograph to point to the particular piece of the project that you want the interviewer to see. Of course, including a short note next to the arrow would also help.

Yet another section in your portfolio might have an official copy of your college transcripts, if they were good enough to be of note.

The above paragraphs mention several sections that you could have in your portfolio. And, of course, depending upon the type of work you do, there could be any number of other sections. The main thing is that your portfolio should be reflective of who you are and what you do.

In the back pocket of your portfolio you could have your master application, a notepad, and anything else you feel you might need.

With all that said, let me now share a final thought. Even though you put all the work, effort, and money into developing it, and even though you conscientiously remember to bring it with you to every interview, you will not get to show it during every interview.

Most job seekers only get to show their portfolios to about half the folks they interview with. Even so, you should always let interviewers know that you have it, and if something in it will help to answer a question, let them know that you could show them an example. But, always let them make the decision as to whether they want to see it.

The thing to remember is that it won't do you any good if you force it on them. They have to want to see it.

Chapter Twenty-four

Message to Military Personnel

Military experience can be a fantastic help to you in acquiring civilian employment. However, there are a few things that you must keep in mind, especially if most, or all, of your work experience was with Uncle Sam. Probably the most important thing to remember is that you think and act differently than everybody else.

The way this shows the most is in your vocabulary. All employers have acronyms and terms that are specific to them. The military, however, takes first prize in this area. Realizing this, it is imperative that you do whatever is necessary to learn the lingo that your civilian counterparts use.

Some suggestions to help you in this endeavor would be to read any civilian trade magazines that you can get your hands on, attend civilian professional associations, take college classes, actively network with civilian personnel, and secure a civilian mentor. These are just a few ideas, but they are enough to help you get started.

The suggestions in the previous paragraph won't do you much good if you read, attend meetings, and talk with folks in a passive sort of way. You will need to be actively involved if your efforts are going to pay off. As you hear words and phrases that are different than you've been taught, jot them down and practice saying them!

Naturally, you'll want to scrutinize your resume, cover letter, and all other correspondence also. It won't do you much good to be able to talk the talk if your resume doesn't get you in the door to afford you that opportunity.

A couple of examples might be worthwhile here. One young Human Resource professional I know used to think that "logistics" was how the military moved tanks around on a battlefield. Therefore, when screening resumes for a purchasing position, that word simply didn't seem relevant. Until that person learned the difference, resumes indicating experience in logistics were put in the "no" pile!

Military personnel with logistics experience could have made it through that screening process had they simply gone to the effort to "civilianize" the vocabulary on their resumes. For that particular position, all they had to do was use the specific words that were in the job advertisement. The same young H.R. professional developed the ad and you can bet it didn't include the word "logistics."

Another example is especially worthy of mention, as I have personally seen several hundred of you make the following mistake in regard to mentioning your rank. Numbers and letters have very little meaning to most non-military personnel. Therefore, when you say that you were an "E-5," it is meaningless to most of us. If you are going to mention your rank, use words that we will understand, such as sergeant, corporal, or captain. If you were in the military for several years and are still a private, then you probably won't want to mention your rank.

Besides your vocabulary, your posture and everything else is very likely to be more rigid and stiff than what is desired in the civilian world. You must remember that during the interview stage, most employers are looking for a fit. Therefore, relax, smile, have fun, and be yourself! (This does not mean that it's OK to slouch!)

Unbelievably, over the years I have spoken with a few hiring personnel who believe that people coming out of the military aren't very good at making decisions or at thinking for themselves. People who think this are under the impression that the military makes all the decisions for you.

In dealing with this perception, I have two recommendations. First of all, determine whether the interviewer thinks this before attempting to deal with it. Secondly, if you are fairly certain that this is the impression of the interviewer, simply answer some of the questions in such a way as to demonstrate your ability to make decisions. Sharing examples of decisions that you've made, and their results, is one way of doing this. One thing you won't want to stress is your proven ability to blindly follow orders, policies, and directives.

Another negative thought that some hiring personnel have is that officers, as well as the higher-ranking non-commissioned officers, are used to merely barking out orders and then having them followed. Such people, they figure, have never had to be concerned with such things as committees, team decisions, and compromise.

If you sense that this is how your interviewer thinks, share some examples of committees and teams that you were on, as well as times when you had to compromise your way in order to incorporate someone else's ideas.

If your title in the military is a non-civilian type of title, it is acceptable to "civilianize" it. In other words, use the position title that is used for non-military folks that do what you do. If your job in the military was totally unique to the military, then do the best you can and then be sure to stress the transferable skills if you are going to have a narrative or "bullets" (not the ones you shoot, but short phrases that describe your duties and responsibilities).

While employers are not legally allowed to screen people out due to continuing military obligations, some do. Therefore, if you are finished with your military service, it might be a good idea to summarize it on your resume with something like the following: "Honorable Discharge with no further military obligations." By mentioning the type of discharge, that sentence also answers for them the manner in which you left the service. If you had a medical or dishonorable discharge, then I'd recommend that you not mention the type of discharge.

Of course, some fields employ many more ex-military personnel than others, and in these fields (such as the airline industry and security), you won't have to be quite so cautious. And, even in industries that are non-military in nature, if you find yourself being interviewed by someone who has served in the military, then by all means swap some stories if you can and build up some rapport. There is a fraternal camaraderie between military people, and there's certainly no reason that you shouldn't take advantage of it during your job search.

Chapter Twenty-five

Job Search Services

In this chapter, we will be discussing three different types of services that can assist you in your job search: professional recruiters, employment counseling services, and temporary agencies. To find out if such services are offered in your area, simply check the classified ads and yellow pages. Of course, with all the advances in communication capabilities today, you don't have to limit yourself to any particular geographic location.

Professional recruiters, or "head hunters," are in the business of recruiting for employers. They typically have many employer contacts and attempt to find the people their contacts need. This service usually costs the employer 30 percent of the selected candidate's first year's salary. In most all cases, the employer pays this fee, not the candidate.

If you can find a professional recruiter to assist you, then go ahead and let him or her do so; however, don't let that be the extent of your job search. For that matter, it should only be a minor part of your efforts. Remember, it's your job search, so you have to accept the ownership for it and make it happen.

For all the help professional recruiters can offer, there is a rather significant downside. A lot of employers do not prefer to work with them. The reason, of course, is that they are so very expensive, especially considering that most of these employers have their own in-house recruiters to do the job.

Furthermore, most employers don't feel that these outside recruiters have the welfare of the employer at heart. The general thought is that they are simply interested in making a sale–namely, filling the vacancy (so they'll get the commission) before someone else fills it.

Another reason that employers typically don't like to work with professional recruiters is that a recruiter becomes a middleman during the salary negotiation stage. Naturally, recruiters try to get you the highest salary possible (since their commission is based on it), which could be good for you, but this really frustrates employers.

One big reason for this frustration is that for recruiters to have done their jobs adequately, the employer will have shared information with them that they would never have shared with a candidate. In attempting to inflate the offer, these out-of-house recruiters can use this information against the employer.

Several employers have shared with me salary negotiation deals that ended up falling through because of the antics of the out-of-house recruiter. This causes employers to not want to work with that particular recruiter again and leaves a bad taste in an employer's mouth concerning you. What's more, once one of these professional recruiters shares your resume with an employer, the employer can't hire you directly; it has to go through the recruiter. So if that recruiter ends up blowing his or her reputation with an employer, your reputation might be shot, too.

Employment counseling services go by many different names. They are basically set up to offer you advice on how to conduct your job search. Some of them offer classes and workshops to assist you. Most have "career indicator" tests, as well as personality tests, to help you figure out who you are and what you should be doing. They also do resume reviews and mock interviews. While these services can be great, be sure to check out their costs beforehand. Several cost thousands of dollars and require you to sign a contract. If such a service ever asks you to sign a contract, or charges anything other than a "per hour" fee, there is an extremely high chance that it isn't legitimate.

Another thing to watch for with these counseling services are the qualifications of the person that you'll be dealing with. Many times it's a social worker, a teacher, or someone with a master's degree in psychology. While these folks might be able to offer some good job search advice, someone who has actually done hiring for a few different employers would be much better.

The social worker and person with a master's degree in psychology would be better qualified to administer the various personality tests, which can also be part of your job search. So, depending upon what it is you need (actual job search skills or tests to figure out what you should be doing, for example) these folks might be just who you need after all. In summary, before investing a lot of money, interview them so that you will know exactly what you are getting and for how much.

Resume reviewers and people that do resume preparation are a dime a dozen. They are usually people who have purchased a resume software package for their home computer, and maybe a book or two on the subject, and therefore think they are qualified to help you with your resume. Teachers will sometimes go into this line of work figuring that their expertise in the areas of spelling and grammar qualify them to help you.

While these people will be able to help you make your resume look nice and ensure that there are no misspellings, unless they have actually been in the position of weeding through stacks of resumes to make real hiring decisions, they really can't offer the skills and expertise that you need.

There are times, though, when it is perfectly acceptable to use their services. For example, if you don't have access to a computer, then you should have one of these folks design your resume. A resume done with a regular typewriter simply can't compete in today's world where everyone else has his done on a computer. Besides, customization is so much easier when using a computer.

If you do decide to work with such a business, one thing to be careful of is that your resume is your resume—it should be unique to you. This means the look of it as well as the stuff it says. One of the problems with these businesses is that all the resumes they produce look alike, and often-times they even use the same wording for similar jobs that their different clients have held. As someone who has reviewed hundreds of resumes let me tell you, this becomes pretty obvious and does not impress the employer.

Throughout this book I have mentioned and recommended tax-funded operations such as Job Service. These usually offer both professional recruiter services as well as employment counseling services.

As professional recruiters they do not charge employers, so they don't have that particular downside. However, they typically deal with what many employers think of as the "less desirables" of society such as ex-convicts, welfare recipients, and the chronically unemployed. Because of this, some employers don't list their openings with them; but others do, which is one reason that I continually recommend that you include them as part of your Job Search.

Their employment counseling services are usually available for free and really can be of value to you. Several such offices that I'm familiar with offer regular job search seminars as well as entire resource centers for their job seekers to use. These centers have computers with laser-jet printers, books on every aspect of the job search, postings of current openings, information on local employers, and staff on hand to assist you.

The downside of their employment counseling service is that oftentimes their staff is overworked and therefore cannot give you the quality time you may need. Furthermore, you typically have to accept whoever you are assigned to, and this person may not have ever been a hiring authority with a "real" employer out there in the "real" world.

Universities generally have an employment counseling service for their students and alumni. Sometimes called a "placement office" or "career center", they offer many excellent services and seminars for job seekers. Sometimes they allow people from the community who aren't students or alumni to use the services.

Temporary agencies have really gained in popularity in the last decade. As a matter of fact, some employers actually keep "their" employees only as temporary employees. The word "their" is in quotes because the employee is really in the employ of the temporary agency. Doing this allows a company to adjust the size of its workforce more easily and can significantly reduce paperwork having to do with benefits and payroll.

However, whether an employer hires people as temps and eventually converts them to regular employee status, or just keeps them on as temps, the basic job search piece of advice is the same: Getting hired through a temp agency can be a great idea.

The reason is that once you're "in the door," then you can do whatever you have to do impress the socks off the company so it will keep you. Actually seeing you work is always a better indicator of the type of employee you'll be than any resume, reference check, or interview. Furthermore, it'll be much easier for you to pursue some of the other job search skills mentioned in this book, such as networking and research.

If you are out of work and need to make some money as you conduct your job search, working through a temporary agency can benefit you, too. You can, for example, accept daily assignments as they come along. This way, if you get an interview opportunity, you can simply not accept an assignment on that particular day. What's more, temporary agency personnel are in daily contact with H.R. departments and other hiring managers from around your area, so having them in your network could be a real bonus.

Chapter Twenty-six

Job Search Tests

The interview is a test. Your resume is a test. The reference check is a test. In fact, every single thing you do as part of your job search is a test. There are, however, some "real" tests (or "assessments") that you might have to take. Here is a listing of some of the more common ones along with brief descriptions of their purposes.

- Aptitude tests predict your ability to learn and perform job tasks.
- Skills tests measure your knowledge and ability to perform a job (for example, word processing speed for a clerical job, knowledge of street names and routes for a delivery driver, etc.).
- Foreign language tests measure your ability to speak, write, and read a foreign language.
- Literacy tests measure reading and arithmetic levels.
- Personality tests evaluate mental, emotional, and temperamental makeup (important for jobs like police officer, nuclear plant operator, air traffic controller, etc.).
- Integrity tests evaluate the likelihood of employee theft.
- Physical ability tests measure strength, flexibility, stamina, and speed for jobs that require physical performance.

- Medical tests determine physical fitness to do a job.
- Drug tests show the presence of illegal drugs that could impair job performance or threaten the safety of others.

Now that we know what some of the various employment tests are, let's review some suggestions for preparing for and taking them.

You can't study directly for aptitude tests, but you can get ready to do your best by taking other tests. Look for tests or quizzes in magazines and books. Set time limits. Practice will help you feel comfortable when you are tested during an interview.

Brush up on job skills. For example, if you're taking a typing test, practice typing. If you're taking a construction test, review blueprints and maybe even visit a construction site and visit with the foreman.

Get ready for physical tests by doing activities similar to those required for the job. For literacy tests, review and do exercises in reading and math books, or enroll in remedial classes.

It's natural to be nervous about tests. You can be sure that most of the other people taking the test are nervous, too. Some anxiety may even help you!

The day before the test, make a list of what you need for it (pencil, eyeglasses. identification, etc). Be sure to check this list before leaving for the test.

Here's a smattering of other suggestions:

- Get a good night's sleep and be sure to leave for the test site early.
- If you're sick, call and try to reschedule.
- If you have any physical difficulties, tell the test administrator.
- If you don't understand the test instructions, ask for help before the test begins.
- Work as fast as you can.
- Don't linger over difficult questions.

- Find out if guessing is penalized. If it's not, guess on questions you're not sure about. You may be able to retake the test.
- Ask about the retesting policy, but realize that your score would probably be similar if you did take the test a second time.
- Finally, after the test, find out what your scores actually mean. See if the test administrators can recommend jobs that your scores show would be best for you.
- And remember, for many jobs and most employers, your work talents and other capabilities, as well as how much they like you, will count more than your test scores.

Chapter Twenty-seven

Professional Statement

You're on the "tour" part of your interview, and as a middle-aged woman walks by, your host introduces you to her. She's the senior vice president of the company, and she asks you to tell her about yourself. It's obvious that she only has a few seconds before she has to continue on her way. What do you say?

You've just finished an eight-hour day of interviews and you're bushed. Wrapping up the last one, you're asked, "So why should we hire you?" or "Do you have any last words that you'd like to leave us with?" What do you say?

You've gone to dinner with your spouse, and as you enter the restaurant you see someone in your network leaving with a colleague. As you pass each other, your contact says that he'd like to introduce you to his friend. You recognize his name as the "all important, big cheese, Grand Pooh-Bah" that he'd promised to introduce you to. You are totally unprepared for this chance meeting. What do you say?

What DO you say? The answer to that question, my friend, is that you say your professional statement.

A professional statement is three to six sentences that summarize your entire professional being. It communicates what you've done with your life, what you can do, and where you are going. It demonstrates that you are filled with such qualities as ambition, integrity, and excellent work ethics. It lets them know that you are excited about the prospect of working for that particular employer. And by having it prepared in advance, it allows you to come across as totally prepared whenever you need something sharp to say about yourself at the spur of the moment.

In any of the three circumstances above, not to mention the infinite number of other circumstances where it could come in handy, how you respond to the question asked could make or break you.

In the first scenario, for example, your host might have been fairly impressed with you up to that point. But if you stammer or mumble something none-too-impressive, his impression of you could plummet. Just think about it–*your* looking bad to that senior vice president could make your host look bad to her, and your host will not appreciate that.

Your professional statement is not something that you jot down in a few minutes. To do it justice, it will take several hours. It should require you to consult with colleagues who know you and who will be honest with you, about you. It should cause you to analyze lists of action words and adjectives to give it a little spice. It needs to be you, while at the same time being a super you.

One way to think about it is to consider what a good friend and professional colleague would say about you to somebody that he hoped might hire you. This would be a good friend who has worked with you for several years and maybe even went to college with you. He knows your strengths and weaknesses.

And he knows you personally, too, so he knows your personal characteristics. And this is a friend who really believes in you and really believes that the job he hopes to help you get is a perfect fit. What would that friend say? If he only had three minutes to "sell" you to his colleague, how would he do it?

Depending upon your individual strengths, your professional statement might have one or two sentences on each of the following:

- Overall introduction that includes your name
- Education or academic background

- Professional work experience
- A "success story" or two
- Special certifications, awards, etc.
- Personal attributes and characteristics
- Ambitions and goals
- Reason for your particular interest in the company you're speaking about

Please note that there are at least eight different areas that you could choose. This does not mean that you could end up with a 16-sentence professional statement. After completing the exercises mentioned below, you should choose three to six sentences that best "sell" you, and use only those. Your professional statement will lose its effectiveness if it's too long.

Do not start working on your professional statement by attempting to write an actual paragraph. Start by putting each of the above areas at the top of separate sheets of paper. Then, brainstorm for a few days. List every idea that comes to you under each of the various headings. This is not a time to be humble. At this point don't worry about writing out sentences. Simply put single words or a few key words that'll help you to remember that particular item. Be sure to ask family, friends, and professional contacts to help you develop these lists. It could also be beneficial to review old performance appraisals for ideas.

Once you have your lists, then go through and highlight the best two or three items on each page. Once you have done that, then begin to develop your sentences—making good use of action words and adjectives.

When you have two or three sentences for each of the eight headings listed, then figure out which are the best mix to put into your professional statement. Here's an example of a professional statement.

> Hello, I'm Lark Adkins and I have over six years' experience as a CPA. My bachelor's degree is in administrative

management and all of my graduate-level work is in accounting. Having worked in both the private and public sectors, I can offer you a well-rounded professional background. It may sound strange, but I've always enjoyed working with numbers, so I love the field I'm in. This company's proactive involvement in new technology particularly excites me and so I'm really looking forward to coming to work for you soon!

The above example has a total of five sentences. However, it covers seven of the eight suggested areas mentioned earlier. Specifically, the first sentence covers the first and fifth area mentioned, the second and third sentences cover the second and third areas, the fourth sentence touches on the sixth area, and the final sentence alludes to the seventh area and ends with the eighth.

Your professional statement should be a "living" document. This means that as you use it, you'll need to "tweak" it every so often to improve it. And, of course, you'll want to customize it for whichever employer you are interviewing with.

When you use it, it needs to flow and sound natural. Do not let it sound like a canned speech! This will require a lot of out-loud practice, but if it's going to work, it'll be worth the effort. And the more you put into it, the more you'll get out of it! It's got to sound like the real you, so be yourself when you use it.

Having a professional sentence is also a good idea. This would basically be your response whenever you're asked the question, "What do you do?" This sentence won't "sell" you like the professional statement, but in many situations it is more appropriate than the full paragraph. It's a quick little response that you can provide without hesitation. It's an opportunity to promote your job search without being at a loss for words or apologetic about your situation. Examples include: "I'm an excellent oral hygienist and I'm looking for a job," or "I've had a successful career as a manufacturing supervisor, but right now I'm looking for something in restaurant management."

Chapter Twenty-eight

Blind Ads

To begin with, let's define "blind ads." These are the help-wanted ads where the employer doesn't include its name and address. Employers typically place these ads in one of two ways. The first is to purchase a blind box through the newspaper in which it's advertising. When this is done, all responses are directed to that box, in care of the newspaper, and the paper forwards the responses on to the employer. The other way companies place such ads is to simply use their own post office address, with no further information that would clue you in as to the name and street location of the employer.

Let's analyze the reasons that an employer uses blind ads. Obviously, one reason is so that it isn't inundated with phone calls and follow-up letters. It is not uncommon for an employer to receive hundreds of responses to a position advertisement, and having to deal with two or three calls or letters from each of these applicants can eat up a lot of hours.

Another reason employers use blind ads is when they are in the process of replacing someone who doesn't yet know that he is being replaced. An employer might be anticipating an opening and is simply in the process of proactively checking out the market and interest level. The important thing here is to remember that the employer chose to run the ad as a blind ad for a reason, and if you hope to be successful in your job search, you must be sensitive to that reason.

You may be asking if the company placed an ad as a blind ad, why bother going to the trouble of finding out who it is? The answer is that you must remember that while the company has the position, from your perspective, it's your job search and career that we're talking about. By finding out who the company is, you could impress the employer with your creativity and diligence.

Many employers would assume that if you're the type of person to go the extra mile in you job search, then you're probably the type of individual to go the extra mile on the job, too. Another reason is that you could discover that it's an employer you wouldn't want to work for. Another reason they place blind ads is to cover a bad reputation, thus enabling them to receive applications and resumes from quality candidates who wouldn't apply otherwise!

Another question that you might be asking is, "Won't I upset an employer by trying to uncover its identity?" The answer here is entirely based upon how you use the information. As mentioned previously, you must be sensitive to the employer's reason for placing the ad. Being discerning is extremely important at this stage in your job search.

Some employers may not object to one or two applicants walking in. Otherwise, you could simply put the company's name on your letter, letting the employer know that you did your homework, yet showing that you are still going through the channels they laid out. A third option on how you use the information is to simply find out for your own knowledge, and then respond to the ad as though you didn't know. This way, you would be in a better position to tailor your cover letter, and even customize your resume, to the employer's particular need.

With all that said, let's now look at some ways to discover a company's identity. For ads where the companies list their own post office address, you could simply call the post office. The post office will usually tell you, provided that the box belongs to a business and not to an individual.

If you can't find out that way, you may have to do some serious legwork. After picking up your Sherlock Holmes pipe, you can begin by pulling whatever information you can about the employer from the ad. Most blind ads will say something about the employer, such as: "a mid-sized, non-union, computer manufacturer in the Northwest," or "a large, privately owned food distributor with locations nationwide." The ZIP code they use will significantly reduce the area in which you'll have to look.

Another thing to do is to go to your local library and look in major newspapers around the country. If the company advertised in only one paper, then it's a fairly safe bet that the position, and thus the employer, is close to that city. If the employer advertised in several papers, this will give you an idea of the region in which to look. Furthermore, by looking in various papers, you might learn more about the employer because an employer will sometimes customize the ad to whichever market it's attempting to reach. Employers will occasionally place blind ads in some papers and include their name and address in others.

With the information you've gained from following the above suggestions, you are now equipped to go looking for the companies. You could start by reviewing the phone books for the area in which you believe they may be located. Another thing to do would be to contact the City Council offices for specific cities and inquire about companies that fit what you've learned from the ads and other sources. You could also network, contacting similar employers and asking who they know who might be looking to fill such a position.

If the employer used the newspaper's confidential box service, then you most assuredly will have to follow the investigation techniques mentioned above, because it's highly unlikely that the newspaper would share the employer's name and address with you. Although, it certainly wouldn't hurt to try—the worst the newspaper could say is no.

There are many other ways to discover who the employer is, but the main thing is to be creative, stay positive, be diligent, and above all else, be discerning once you do discover who it is!

Does this actually work? Absolutely! I've successfully coached several clients on how to do this. One such time, an ad appeared that looked very promising, mentioning that the successful candidate would be spending summers in Sun Valley (a resort town), and winters in Montana. One client was intrigued and wanted to know more; however, there was no indication of who the employer was.

We decided that he owed it to himself to find out more. Early one morning he showered, shaved, got dressed up in his best interview suit, and drove the couple hundred miles to Sun Valley. Once he got there, he had to do several hours of investigative work, as well as make about a dozen long-distance phone calls to Montana, but by the end of the day, he was able to walk into the employer's office!

At the front desk, he said, "I'll bet you've received hundreds of resumes for your position, but I'll bet I'm the only one to walk in to apply. Does this earn me an interview?" The woman who happened to be up front was one of the hiring managers and said that she certainly thought it should. Not long into the interview it was very obvious that the opportunity wasn't such a wonderful match after all and he thanked them for their time and departed.

Reflecting on that experience, we realize that had he not done what he did, he would never have been called for an interview, because his resume was one of hundreds and not really a good match anyway. But he would have always wondered about that particular opportunity. Rather than passively sitting by and allowing his job search to be defined by others, he chose to take the proactive stance and maintain control of his career. It's not that difficult and you can do it, too!

Chapter Twenty-nine

Dealing With Prejudice

Don't you hate it when you go in to an interview and you can just tell that the interviewer immediately stereotypes you–putting you in the same category as how he might perceive others of your age, gender, nationality, weight, etc? For example, maybe you are a 62-year-old looking for a career position, or perhaps a young black man looking forward to a new challenge, or maybe a woman looking to re-enter the workforce after several years of furlough. In each of these situations, you could easily find yourself facing an interviewer who might have certain biases against you simply because of your age, color, or gender.

What do you do? Sure, you can talk to people who know the law and they'll be able to quote chapter and verse of the laws stating that such discrimination is illegal. But we both know that it still happens. Or you can take advantage of the sad fact that our country has become a "sueciety," and take the company to court, but that just ties up your time, and you still don't have a job. Another option is to let promising employment opportunities pass you by, but this certainly isn't the option of choice either.

Why don't we tackle this very real problem head-on? Let's first realize that most interviewers are not really down-to-the-core prejudiced. The ones who are will eventually be found out and they will be dealt with, either by their employer or by one or more of the many regulatory agencies that our government has to protect us from such people. And besides, as you've probably already heard elsewhere, you wouldn't really want to work at a place that tolerated such bigotry.

This leaves us with ordinary people with ordinary biases, and we can deal with these. The first thing to do is to take a look at whatever group you are being associated with (whether the association is accurate or not) and objectively list negative concerns that are associated with that group. Remember, the question here is not whether you are these things. The question is, how might others perceive a person in that group.

If you have difficulty being objective, or developing such a list, you could always solicit assistance from friends and co-workers. I would recommend that you include friends and co-workers who belong to other groups (gender, race, age, weight) than the one to which you are perceived to belong. In recent years, diversity training has become very popular and one of the exercises that a trainer often uses is to name a group of people and have the audience offer thoughts that come to mind when people think of that group.

For example, responses to the question "Older people are sometimes thought of as...?" could include: low-energy, forgetful, can't learn new stuff, slow, health problems, stuck on doing things the old way, won't stay for very long, etc.

Now, regardless of whether you agree with these thoughts, let me ask you a question. How likely do you think it is that an interviewer would come right out and ask an applicant about these things? Unless the interviewer has absolutely no common sense at all, he won't! Yet, if the interviewer has such biases, he will tend to rate you lower simply because he thinks you have certain characteristics.

What can you do about this? The answer is to knock down those false arguments without them ever being asked. You do this by creatively offering little tidbits here and there as opportunity allows. Basically, you answer the unasked questions!

This can be done in answer to certain questions or as part of the "small talk" that generally precedes or follows an interview. As a last resort, you could even mention the little tidbits in your thank you letter! The earlier in the process that you knock down these obstacles, the better chance you will have to get the job offer.

What little tidbits am I talking about? If you are an older person facing the negative perceptions mentioned earlier, you could effectively eliminate the low-energy, slow, and health problems concerns by being sure to tell the interviewer about your active participation in whatever sport club or activity you regularly join in. If you play volleyball every week, take karate lessons, go hiking with the local Boy Scout troop, or even golf on a regular basis you'll be telling the interviewer loud and clear that you have high energy, aren't slow, and have good health.

You can attack the perceptions that you might be forgetful, can't learn new stuff, and are stuck on doing things the old way by sharing something new you've learned recently. If you are currently or have recently been enrolled in any sort of college course or seminar, this will speak volumes as to your mental aptitudes and overall attitude.

If you are not actively participating in some activity or taking classes somewhere, you might consider doing so. Another option is to take a good look at what you are doing and figure out how it could translate into knocking down these negative perceptions.

The final negative perception mentioned, concerning the thought that you may not stay for very long, can be addressed by mentioning your future goals. You should know that employers today are considerably different than employers of 30 years ago. These days, if employers can get three good years out of an employee, they feel they've broken even, and anything beyond that is more than they were bargaining for in the first place.

While I have used age bias as the example for this chapter, the same idea holds true for racial, gender, weight, and other forms of prejudice. While it is difficult to deal with such issues due to their subliminal nature, these techniques should equip you to have a better chance at achieving that dream job that you've been hoping for.

And as a reminder, you must stay positive when conducting a job search. If you allow other people's biases, and even rejections, to affect you personally, other employment offers will be affected due to your attitude. And only you are capable of controlling that!

Chapter Thirty

Creating Your Own Fast-Track

We've all heard of those major corporations with official fast-track programs for their up-and-coming stars. But what do you do if you don't work for a company that offers such a program? Or maybe your employer offers a fast-track program, but you haven't been selected to participate in it. This can be frustrating, causing unneeded stress and anxiety.

Rather than passively accepting the situation, I'd like to suggest that you create your own fast-track. By taking control of your career, you'll reduce your stress and anxiety and replace it with the optimism that comes with stretching yourself to reach your own professional goals. As someone once said, "...to reach for the goals you have set for yourself...that is success."

How does one do this? The first thing you must do is to set realistic goals. If you are currently a clerk, it is probably unlikely that will be vice president in two years. Even official fast-track programs generally take several years and many different positions before the "star" has the knowledge, skills, abilities and contacts to succeed in the more prestigious positions. And remember, these are people who are recognized as being shining stars up front. If you haven't been selected for the program, or if your employer doesn't have such a system set up, you may have to position yourself properly before anyone takes proper notice of you.

How do you set these goals? You should begin by figuring out what you'd truly like to do for a living. Please don't limit yourself by the dream job's earning potential. In other words, don't decide not to pursue a certain long-term professional goal simply because the position doesn't typically earn as much as you hope to be earning. Enjoying what you are doing for a living is much more important than any salary. You also don't want to rule out a position due to it being too "high in the sky." Some positions may take 10 or 20 years to achieve, but if it's what you truly want, you should go for it. The services of a competent career counselor might be very advantageous to you at this point.

Once you know where you want to be, take a look at the types of knowledge, skills and abilities that such a position would require. You can do this by reviewing the professional histories of current, as well as past, incumbents. You could also talk to someone in your Human Resource Department or a manager in the particular area in which you hope to be employed some day.

When you have an idea of what the position requires, put together an outline of how you can get those prerequisites. You may need to attend some seminars, take some college courses, or even pursue a degree. Aside from academics, begin looking for positions that will give you some practical, real-life experience. You may need to accept a lower paying job, or even one that you dislike, and work it for a year or two, but remember, what you are doing is paying the price. It may take being in the trenches for a while before upper management begins to take notice. You may also have to change employers in order to get the experience you need.

Another absolute necessity is your attitude. You're not likely to be considered for a higher-level position if you are known as one who can't follow directions, criticizes management, or can't get along with co-workers. You will also need to have an impeccable attendance record. This may include coming in to work a half-hour early every day or staying a half-hour later. The people at the top typically didn't make it there by working 8 to 5, five days per week. They got there by burning the midnight oil and continuing to improve themselves while at the same time being of value to their employer.

Mentoring has become extremely popular in the last decade or so, and you can bet that just about every fast-track program incorporates it into its agenda. Creating your own fast-track program, you should include it, too. It not only allows you to learn from your mentor, but your mentor could be a great ally down the road when you need a reference or contact.

Selecting the right mentor is extremely important. You want someone who is recognized as a success, as well as someone that you respect and trust. You should be sure to ask the person if she would consent to being your mentor, and then you should be willing to follow her advice.

I would also recommend letting certain people know about your future goals and plans. This can help you immensely if they are in a position to give you opportunities. For example, in my first H.R. job, I let my manager know that I eventually hoped to go into international Human Resources. She knew I was serious because I was enrolled in graduate level H.R. courses at the local university.

Shortly after informing her of my goals, she began to ask me to wine and dine the managers that we would fly in from our overseas facilities! I absolutely loved the opportunity to discuss international H.R. with these people, and the managers from our facility liked it because it meant that they didn't have to give up an evening with their families.

And guess what? While she was helping to groom me for where I wanted to go, I gave her and the company everything I had to offer because I knew that they cared about me.

Another time or two, the H.R. manager arranged for me to work with the H.R. manager from our European operations. You can bet that I appreciated that, put my best foot forward, and even (after building some rapport) let the H.R. manager of European operations know of my intentions to be working for him in a few years!

Aside from technical grooming, you might want to work on other areas, too. For example, you could read Dale Carnegie's books. You could also do things to improve your reading abilities, vocabulary, and professional image.

Knowing where you want to go, developing a plan to get there, and then pursuing it can be extremely satisfying and rewarding. Another thing to keep in mind these days, with companies laying people off, is that if you are let go, you should see it as an opportunity to progress and improve yourself, an opportunity to gain new experiences and increase your network of contacts. Try not to burn any bridges, stay positive, and take control of your career!

Chapter Thirty-one

Job Search Evaluation

Throughout your job search, you should be altering it to improve your effectiveness. Hopefully, you'll secure a position right away, and your feedback (having been offered a job) will let you know that you were doing a good job. However, if your job search drags on for months and months, it might be in need of an overhaul.

Of course, you don't want to wait for months before determining its effectiveness. One natural time to review your efforts is immediately after every interview. To assist you in your self-evaluation, try asking yourself these questions:

- What points did I make that seemed to interest the employer?
- Did I present my qualifications well?
- Did I overlook any important qualifications?
- Did I learn all I needed to know about the position?
- Did I ask all the questions I had about the position?
- Did I talk too much? Too little?
- Was I too tense? Too relaxed?
- Was I too aggressive? Too passive?
- Was I dressed appropriately?
- Did I close the interview effectively?
- What would I do differently if I could do it over?

Make a list of specific ways you could improve your next interview. Practice makes perfect and the more you interview, the better you will get.

Aside from asking yourself the above questions after every interview, you should be constantly reviewing the other aspects of your job search, too. At least weekly, you should review all you have accomplished as a way of helping you decide whether to step up the pace. If you do go several months without some good job offers, then it would probably behoove you to hire a job search consultant for some professional advice. To this end, check out *www.jobsearchadvisor.com.*

If that isn't practical or possible for you, then at the very least, re-read this book and figure out where the hitch is. If you're only applying at one place per month, then you'll need to set more aggressive goals or expand your search area. If you're sending out lots of resumes, but not getting invited for interviews, then it could be a problem with your resume. If you're being invited in for lots of interviews, and simply aren't getting the offers, then it could be your references or the interview itself.

The chapter on references offers some advice on how to determine if that's a problem area, and what to do about it if it is. If it's not your references, then it's probably your interview. If that's the case, then it might be a good time to arrange a mock interview. At this point in your job search, having several interviews behind you, you should try to remember which questions have been asked by more than one employer, and then be sure that those questions are asked during the mock interview.

Having the mock interview videotaped would be most beneficial, especially if it's a friend who's acting as the interviewer, as opposed to somebody who does it for a living. Later, while watching yourself on video, ask yourself if you'd hire this person. Be sure to consider your body language as well as what you say. Make note of any weaknesses, and then practice until you overcome them.

Chapter Thirty-two

Investing in Your Future

A proper job search requires certain investments—two to be exact: time and money. Of course, if you're still with me at this point in the book, you've undoubtedly figured this out for yourself by now. If you don't have an overabundance of either of these two commodities, all is not lost. Simply prioritize and cut corners where and when you can.

Job search expenses include, but are definitely not limited to, the following: resumes (to get them initially created as well as for each subsequent print), special paper for your cover letters and thank you letters, postage, professional associations and other groups (membership fees as well as luncheon expenses), research (to get a newspaper to do a search for you, for example), telephone charges, travel expenses, dry cleaning, shoe shines, haircuts, and clothing. The financial investment could be even more substantial if your job search plans include professional seminars, some college courses, or a degree.

A proper job search takes a lot of time, too. If you are out of work, it can take up all your time, and it should if your number one priority is to get another job. You need to spend at least 40 to 60 hours per week actively pursuing employment.

If you are ambitious and are really looking to grow in your professional career, then the time investment could take on some additional dynamics. For example, you might have to open yourself up to consideration of previously undesirable options as well as to some personal growth and change. Typically, however, such drastic measures end up yielding significant returns.

Remember, if you're looking for a job, then you're working for yourself. If you were paying someone $20, $50, or $100 per hour, you'd expect him to use his time wisely. Why expect anything less from yourself. So get after it! Take charge of your search—go out there and get a job!

Part III

The REAL Decision-Maker

Chapter Thirty-three

The REAL Decision-Maker With Job Search Examples

When I do seminars on job search skills, or when I do one-on-one counseling on the subject, people can generally tell that I enjoy sharing this information that I've learned the hard way. And I do enjoy it, because I absolutely love to help people. That seems to be one of my big motivators.

However, there is another subject that I get even more excited about sharing. And, as luck would have it, any discussion on job search skills would be thoroughly incomplete without it. You can do all of the things that have been outlined in this book and still be extremely unsuccessful in your job search. As a matter of fact, I've often heard myself say that all of this stuff adds up to only a very small percentage of the reason for being successful in looking for employment.

What makes up the larger percent? Well, it has been my experience that my close and personal relationship with the Lord, Jesus Christ, is what really determines my success in my job searches as well as in every other area of my life. Since this is a book on job searches, let me share some real-life examples of how He has worked and has been active in a few of my job searches.

The first one I'll share has to do with how I once got a job when the employment opportunities were especially bleak. It happened well after I'd accepted the Lord as my Savior, but at that time, as well as for several years before that, I wasn't living the life that He would have wanted me to be living. But even though I wasn't actively pursuing Him, He was watching out for me, and was being patient with me till I turned back to Him, much like the father waiting for the prodigal son.

At the time, I really liked the town I was living in, but the job market was about nil, and I was out of work. While I wasn't trying to grow spiritually, I was attending church simply because it was the social thing to do.

One time, I happened to mention to some folks at the church that I needed to find a job or would have to move to a larger city that offered more employment opportunities. That next Sunday, the pastor told the entire congregation. I'm the type of person that doesn't like to air my personal business to everyone else, so this really upset me. The nerve of him to share my personal situation with the entire congregation!

As a matter of fact, I was so mad that I didn't hear a single word the pastor said throughout the sermon because my fists were clinched, and I was planning to hit him as soon as the service was over. Really!

Immediately after the service, I was making my way down to see the pastor when a man stepped in front of me and told me about how he could get me on with his employer. His employer was one of the most reputable companies in the area, and within two weeks I had the job.

This was nothing short of a miracle. I knew nothing about that guy's industry, yet God provided a job anyway. Furthermore, even though I wasn't looking to learn any lessons, He managed to teach me a thing or two about opening up a bit and letting the people from the church help me. He sure does work in mysterious ways!

The second job search in which God most assuredly helped me was when I was interviewing for my first position in Human Resources. At that point in my life, I was beginning to realign myself with His desires for my life, and He stepped in and helped me get a position that was in a town that had a great church. A church that ended up really helping me get back on track with the Lord.

The first way He helped was to get me in for the initial screening interview. More than 300 people had applied for the position, most of which far exceeded the qualifications, and I didn't even meet the minimum qualifications!

The second way He helped was with my final interview. I had done fairly well in the first couple; however, I totally blew the final one that just happened to be with the top executive in the company. I did so poorly that after following him out of his office, he walked back toward the factory and I headed for the exit that was in the opposite direction. Just as I was walking out the door, he called to me from about 40 feet away saying, "Where are you going? You need to be following me."

Needless to say, he couldn't have thought much of yours truly. I'd screwed up the interview and then hadn't followed him like I was supposed to, ending up looking fairly dumb because he had to call to me from a distance. However, when you have connections with the Creator of the universe, miracles can and do happen! That guy may have run that entire international corporation, but my Heavenly Father wanted me to have that job, so I got it. For Jesus Christ, 300 to 1 odds are nothing!

A third time that God definitely had a direct hand in my obtaining employment was when I managed to get a senior-level H.R. position with the government. This time, I was relying on Him and trusted Him to provide me with the job that He would want me to have. This meant that I was earnestly praying before every interview asking for His help and sharing that I only wanted the position if it was His will. If it wasn't His will, then I did not want the job.

And I meant it. For example, I got really close on one really good job and had other people praying with and for me (notice that I'd learned from the earlier experience). After I didn't get the offer, several of these people mentioned that they were sad for me. My honest and sincere response was, "Thank God I didn't get the offer because it obviously wasn't the job He wanted for me, and if it wasn't the job He wanted for me, then I certainly didn't want it!" And deep down, that really is how I felt. I truly had given Him control of my job search!

Then two government positions were advertised, both of which were with the same department. Either one would have been fine with me, though one was much better than the other. Six months prior to these positions being advertised, I had absolutely no interest in a position in the public sector. However, at that point in my job search, I really needed a job, so I was open to new ideas. I am confident that this was all part of His great plan.

The government has a rather intense selection process but I managed to qualify for both positions anyway. When I arrived at the office for my interview for the better position, rather than begin an interview, the interviewers took me to an office and gave me a problem to solve in 45 minutes. Afterward, they would interview me.

Taking one took at the problem, I knew I was in trouble. I hadn't a clue what to do. Reviewing the problem, I realized that I had absolutely no idea of what format the answer was supposed to be in. Did they want me to draw a chart? Write out an answer in narrative? Would the answer be a number? I had no idea. I was so lost that I couldn't even ask questions because I didn't know what to ask!

Now, are you ready to hear an amazing story on the power of prayer? Before every interview, I had always prayed, asking for His guidance and asking for an offer, only if it was a position that He would want me to have. Well, prior to my interview for this better position, I had forgotten to pray.

Shortly after looking at the problem, I realized that I hadn't prayed. So I bowed my head and did it, asking for His assistance. I again mentioned that I only wanted the position if it was the position that He wanted me to have, but I asked Him to please help me not to look totally stupid. After all, there was that other position with the same department and if I totally flubbed up this interview, it would certainly affect my chances at that position also.

Within seconds after finishing that prayer, I suddenly knew how to work the problem and what the interviewers wanted as far as a finished product. It was truly scary! Figuring that God must have reached down and put the information into my brain, I actually turned around in my chair fully expecting to see God's hand leaving the room. Or I figured I'd see Rod Serling from *The Twilight Zone*. Anyway, I finished the problem in the time remaining and was then able to explain and justify my answer during the interview! And, yes, I ended up getting the job.

Chapter Thirty-four

Establishing a Relationship With the Real Decision-Maker

Will He do for your job search what He has done for mine? I don't know, but what I do know is that it certainly is possible. Does this mean that you should hit your knees and start praying for a job? Not necessarily.

Before you go to Him for assistance, you really need to look at what you've done with what He's already done for you. What He's done is that He sent His only Son to pay the price for your sins. If you haven't accepted His Son, then why should you think that you would experience His plan for your life?

If you answer that last question with, "because He loves everybody," you would only be partially correct. Yes, He does love everybody because He is a loving God. However, He is also a just God, and His justice requires the payment of a price. And only Jesus can pay that price. So what you do with Him, will determine what He does with you—not only on your job search, but also with the much more important issue of your eternal life.

Am I telling you to stop all the bad habits that you currently enjoy? Am I telling you to start attending a church? Am I telling you to start doing a whole bunch of good things? NO! Those things will come once He's in your life. What I'm telling you is to acknowledge your sin, turn from it, ask for forgiveness, accept Him as your personal Savior, and then begin to develop a personal relationship with Him. That's what He wants.

How do you do this? Here are four steps that answer that question:

1. RECOGNIZE GOD'S PLAN

   God loves you and created you to know Him personally. The Bible says, "For God so loved the world that He gave His only begotten Son, so that whoever believes in Him should not perish, but have eternal life." *John 3:16*

2. REALIZE OUR PROBLEM–SEPARATION

   People choose to disobey God and go their own way. This results in separation from God. The Bible says, "For all have sinned and fall short of the glory of God." *Romans 3:23* And it goes on to say, "For the wages of sin is death" (spiritual separation from God). *Romans 6:23*

3. RESPOND TO GOD'S REMEDY–JESUS CHRIST'S DEATH

   God sent His Son to bridge the gap. Christ did this by paying the penalty of our sins when He died on the cross and rose from the grave. Jesus says, "I am the way, and the truth, and the life; no one comes to the Father, but through Me." *John 14:6*

   The Bible goes on to say, "But God demonstrates His own love toward us, in that while we were yet sinners, Christ died for us." *Romans 5:8*

4. RECEIVE GOD'S SON–LORD AND SAVIOR

   You cross the bridge into God's family when you ask Christ to come into your life. The Bible says, "As many as received Him, to them He gave the right to become children of God." *John 1:12* The Bible goes on to say that we are saved by grace, not by works (good deeds). *Ephesians 2:8,9.* And, it quotes Jesus as saying, "Behold, I stand at the door and knock. If anyone hears My voice and opens the door, I will come in." *Revelation 3:20*

The invitation is to repent (turn from your sins) and by faith receive Jesus Christ into your heart and life and follow Him as your Lord and Savior.

If this sounds like something you'd like to do, here's a simple prayer of commitment:

> "Dear Lord Jesus, I know I am a sinner. I believe You died for my sins. Right now, I turn from my sins and open the door of my heart and life. I receive You as my personal Lord and Savior. Thank You for saving me now. Amen."

If you just prayed that prayer (or whenever you do in the future), then you are (or will be) a child of God! You may want to remember this as your "spiritual birthday." If so, record the date and your initials here:

Chapter Thirty-five

The Next Step–Developing the Relationship

Here are some recommendations that will help you to grow as a Christian:

- Thank God every day that He will never leave you. "For He Himself has said, 'I will never desert you nor will I ever forsake you.'" *Hebrews 13:5*

- Abide in Christ; seek to know Him personally. Keep Him first place in your life.
  "Abide in Me, and I in you. As the branch cannot bear fruit of itself, unless it abides in the vine, so neither can you, unless you abide in Me." *John 15:4*

- Pray. Talk to God every day about everything. "Casting all your anxiety upon Him, because He cares for you." *I Peter 5:7*

- Read your Bible daily. "But He answered and said, 'it is written, man shall not live on bread alone, but on every word that proceeds out of the mouth of God.'" *Matthew 4:4* (The Gospel of John is a great book to start with.)

- "Be filled with the (Holy) Spirit." *Ephesians 5:18* This means to allow the Holy Spirit to direct and empower your life. In your prayers, confess all known sin regularly. "If we confess our sins, He is faithful and righteous to forgive us our sins and to cleanse us from all unrighteousness." *I John 1:9*

- Worship God regularly. "Not forsaking our own assembling together, as is the habit of some, but encouraging one another; and all the more, as you see the day drawing near." *Hebrews 10:25*
- Obey God. "Jesus answered him, 'If anyone loves Me, he will keep My Word.'"
  John 14:23
- Meditate on God's word, maybe even memorizing a favorite verse or two. My favorite verse is *Matthew 22:37-40.*

When you're looking for a church home, I'd recommend that you find a Christian church that believes in the Bible. I know that most churches profess this, but one way to know for sure is to see if the pastor actually teaches out of the Bible, as opposed to just telling stories that vaguely relate to concepts that are in the Bible.

When looking for a church home, another thing to beware of is any group that accepts any other book as equal in authority with the Bible. There is only one Bible, and it begins with Genesis and ends with the book of Revelation. You will also want to steer clear of any groups that do not accept Jesus Christ as God's only begotten Son. As the Bible clearly states, believing in Jesus Christ is the only way to secure eternal life. As such, He is the One we pray to—we do not pray to His mother, the apostles, or anyone else. And since Jesus Christ is the only way to be saved, we are saved by faith, not by works, as mentioned in *Ephesians 2:8-9.*

Another thing that you will want in a church home is for it to be spirit-filled. This can be difficult to ascertain, but one very simplistic way to get a clue as to whether it is spirit-filled is to see how much joy is apparent during its worship time. Do the people smile and seem to actually want to be there? Do they sing out loud and openly welcome newcomers? If so, then there's a good chance that it is a spirit-filled church.

When looking for a new church, I recommend that you look for two things. First and foremost, seek out a church that is Biblically-based and

Scripturally-sound. Secondly, it should be a place where your social needs can be met. Simply put, if your family and you don't like to hang out with the members of the church, then it'll be difficult to develop real relationships with them. Building these relationships will help you to enjoy true fellowship. This fellowship will then allow you to encourage others in their faith as well as allow them to encourage you.

Chapter Thirty-six

My Spiritual Journey—The Authors' Testimony

When I was a child, church was pretty much something that we occasionally had to do with our mom. When I was 9 years old, a friend invited me to his church one evening for an activity for kids our age. When it was time for us to go outside and play, the minister asked me some rather in-depth questions about where I was spiritually. Rather than go and play with the rest of the guys, I stayed behind and listened to what this man had to say about Jesus Christ and what it was to have a real, personal relationship with Him.

He explained to me the fact that God is perfect and that man is not. He said that because of this, man could not be with God because God could not allow imperfection in His presence. The good news, however, was that God did want us to be with him, so he sent his one and only Son, Jesus Christ. Jesus was born as a man, but was perfect-He was God in the flesh! Jesus came to earth to die for our sins. He then explained to me that the only way that anyone could go to be with God and live in heaven forever was to accept Jesus Christ as his personal savior. Basically I had to admit that I was a sinner and that Jesus, who was sinless, died on my behalf (i.e., paid for my sins) so that I could go to heaven. I had to accept Jesus into my heart as my personal savior.

After explaining all this to me, he asked me if I had ever heard of any of this before. I had not. He then asked me if I fully understood everything he had said. I did understand what he had said and I wanted to accept

Jesus as my personal savior. After questioning me a little more, and providing a bit more explanation, so as to be absolutely sure that I understood the ramifications of what Jesus had done, he knelt on the floor with me and led me in prayer to accept Jesus Christ. My spiritual journey became quite turbulent after this, but the fact that I remember that evening so clearly is one reason that I know I truly became a Christian that day.

A couple years later I had a rather unfortunate, negative religious experience. At that time in my life one of my hobbies was magic. I would give magic shows for the neighborhood children, charging about a nickel per kid. When my Sunday School teacher (a young man named Sandy) found out that I liked magic, he told me to stop. He showed me Deuteronomy 18:10-12. I did not make the distinction between the 'black magic' to which this verse refers and the simple little party tricks that I did. After all, you're supposed to trust your Sunday School teacher, aren't you?

Years later when I finally realized that he was wrong about God being against my hobby, I realized the incredible influence that a person in such a position could have on an individual. If I had asked my parents, I'm sure the matter could have been cleared up. However, talking with my parents was not an activity I particularly enjoyed or felt welcome to do at that point in my life. Besides, what was there to ask them? Sandy had said I must stop, so I had to stop, no questions asked. I guess I felt that to question his direction would have been like questioning God. My parents noticed that I suddenly stopped doing magic tricks but didn't find out for years the real reason.

I remember approaching my dad in an attempt to lead him to the Lord when I was in either 5th or 6th grade. This was my first attempt at evangelism. It was not a successful attempt. My dad never really spoke to us kids, so to attempt to talk with him at all was difficult enough. I remember our conversation lasting about as long as a minute before he dismissed me and I fled.

By 7th grade I must have been fairly tuned in to the word of God, because several boys gave me the nickname Bible-Boy. My mom and us kids were attending a church at that time and after an extended study in my Sunday School, our teacher announced that we could join the church. This was my opportunity to participate in Confirmation.

While all the other little 12-year-olds agreed to join, I said, "Wait a minute. This is all I know. How do I know that this is right? How do I know that I believe it? I don't even know what else is out there." So rather than participate in Confirmation, I decided to begin my search for spiritual truth.

I joined an after school Sunday school for Bahai children. I invited the Mormon elders over to review their 7-or 9-week LDS overview. I read about eight books on Tibetan Buddhism written by a monk. Anytime anyone invited me to another church, I accepted. When in airports and on the streets of big cities, I approached religious zealots (like Hare Krishnas) and asked them about their beliefs. In my early 20s when I hitchhiked several thousand miles, the subjects of theology, philosophy, and religious beliefs were a common topic of conversation with the drivers. My spiritual mind was like a sponge absorbing all it could.

My pursuit of truth was not continuous. In the 15-year period between the ages of 12 and 27, there were about three times that I seriously pursued spiritual truths for about a year at a time. My interest was only superficial—I wasn't looking for truth; I was looking for a theology that would allow me to live my life however I wanted to live it. During this time period, I lived by whatever rules I chose. My true lifestyle showed very little proof that I was on a spiritual quest.

Where did all my seeking lead me? It led me to developing my own belief. This belief included the best of all that I'd heard from the various world religions that I'd studied.

Thanks to God and my mom, I had a foundation of Christianity through attending church, various Vacation Bible Schools and a Christian Bible Camp the summers after grades 7 and 8. It was towards the end of my first spiritual quest that I first attended this camp. The camp was great and really made you want to be a Christian. I remember being confused as to whether or not I was a Christian. That first summer, I accepted Christ into my heart for a second and third time. Basically, after sinning I'd feel that my previous acceptance was void, so I'd redo it.

My second summer at camp, I 'accepted Him into my heart' a few more times, because I never felt really sure that He came in. Furthermore, I felt that if He had come in, he probably left after I continued to sin. I was at camp on my birthday when I accepted Him for the last time. I knew that once was all it took, but I'd done it so many times that I felt one last heartfelt acceptance was warranted, and doing it on my birthday would provide me with a date even I could remember.

In hindsight, I now realize that I really wasn't 'accepting Him into my heart' at that camp. I had been a Christian since I was 9 years old. What I did at that camp was to rededicate my life to the Lord several times. These rededications were short-lived as I rapidly returned to whatever lifestyle I chose shortly after leaving camp. But these summers at camp did help to give me a fairly solid foundation in Christ.

The years passed, and then six months after turning 27 I was unemployed and out of money. I was attending a church, and suddenly one Sunday I felt an urge to join. This was significant because I had always planned to wait to join a church until I was married, so my wife and I could join together. Attending and joining a church didn't conflict with my made-up belief because part of my belief was that all religions were correct. Shortly after joining, I began to really rely on the Lord. True need has a way of making people lean towards the one true God.

It was at this time that I realized that my made-up belief was void of any "power" and thus was not capable of helping my situation. At that point in my life I needed something with *real* power! Just when things were about to get desperate, God intervened and gave me a fantastic position with a fabulous company. I say that God intervened because that's exactly what He did. After being hired, I reviewed the 300 resumes that represented the people with whom I was in competition for the one position. There were many people with exactly the desired qualifications. Not only did I not have as much to offer as a lot of individuals, but I totally ruined my final interview with the Plant Manager. It's great when you have God on your side!

The company I went to work for was in the same town where I attended college. One of my old college buddies invited me to a Bible Church one Sunday. This was where I would finally grow up spiritually. The first thing I noticed as we pulled up that night was that there were dozens of good-looking college age people in the parking lot walking towards the church. My first thought was that it must be a cult-I'd never seen a Jesus church with so many people in their late teens and early 20s. Once inside, I really got worried. There were literally hundreds of young people inside. The service was fantastic. After church I wanted to be mad at my friend for not inviting me to this church before.

There were many things that made it so very fantastic. First of all, there was no 'religion' involved. The program went like this: we sang, the preacher preached, we sang, it was over. No robes, no stained glass windows, no pews, no candles. They didn't even take collection! This was a church that trusted God to provide, so once every 3 or 4 months the preacher would mention that there were boxes out in the hallways if folks felt like giving. Finally, this church didn't ask for my name and number, so as to bother me later in the week.

But the best part was the message. The preacher actually preached out of the Bible! I had never seen this before, and I had gone to church all my life. In churches I had attended, the preacher would read a scripture verse or two and then preach on something that might be vaguely related to what he had read. This preacher was preaching right out of the Bible, and the message was actually relevant to my life! This was fantastic!

I decided that I wanted to become a true Christian, with the Bible as my only guide. To do this I realized that I had to pick a real faith religion and forget about my made-up beliefs. This was not an easy thing to do because my mind was totally confused by all the other religious beliefs, philosophies, and theologies that I had opened myself up to.

I made up the following story to describe the dilemma I faced:

> Once there was a man who knew addition and subtraction. With this knowledge, he figured he knew math. Then one day another fellow came by and tried to tell him about multiplication and division. The first man made the sign of the cross as he cried out, "You heathen! That stuff you're talking about is cultic! It's not math, I know math!" However, after a while, the first man did listen and learned to accept that math included all four: addition, subtraction, multiplication, and division.
>
> Then another man came by and wanted to introduce him to algebra. Again he responded with, "You heathen! That stuff you're talking about is cultic! It is not math, I know math! After opening himself up, and listening to the man with an open heart, he came to know that true math included algebra too. This happened again, and again, with the man being leery each time, but eventually learning about geometry, calculus and many other types of math.

My question was, once the man knew and understood all types of math, how could he ever go back to believing that just addition and subtraction were math? In my case, after opening myself up to all the various types of philosophies, theologies, and religious beliefs, how could I ever forget about them and believe only the Bible. I wanted to just believe the Bible, so I would tell my friends that my desire was to become 'close-minded.' My Christian friends said this was a negative way of looking at the situation. They recommended that I refer to it as becoming "focused." I figured the difference was just a matter of semantics, but whichever way you looked at it, my inner desire was to forget all the trash I'd picked up and be a true Christian.

Had I chosen to pursue this goal by myself, there is no doubt in my mind that I would have failed. However, with God's help, through prayer and spending time in the Bible and with other true Christians, I have become focused. It took over a year, but any truly worthwhile endeavor is worth the time and effort it takes to accomplish. Another very important step in my becoming focused was to stop being exposed to other beliefs. Realizing the dire situation my spirituality was in, I took this to the extreme; I would not even visit other Christian churches or discuss theology with anyone who I wasn't absolutely sure believed ONLY the Bible.

I no longer see all those other beliefs as different types of one true discipline. I now see it like this: If Satan wanted to pull people away from the one true God, he would attack on several fronts. He attacks us directly, but he also sneaks in from the rear. One way of doing this would be to start all types of variant beliefs, each with part of the truth, so as to distract people from the one true way to God.

During my years of misguided spiritual quest, I had a very selective memory, choosing to remember only the portions of other beliefs, theologies, and philosophies that supported the particular angle I desired to believe. Because of this, I am not as good as I would like to be, or should be, at evangelizing with folks who adhere to those other beliefs.

After a year and a half of attending that Bible church, I really felt I was living as God would want me to. The best example of this was the fact that just a month after beginning to attend that church, I started treating with respect the girls I would go out with. I truly thought that this was a phenomenal testimony to my changed lifestyle.

While no one can be perfect and live a sinless life, a Christian should make the attempt to live as Christ-like as possible. There were a couple of sins that I continued to wallow in, but I figured they were fairly minor, especially compared to how I used to sin. Also, there was one specific sin that I'd been involved in for over 10 years and had wanted to stop for the last year but wasn't stopping. Knowing that they were sins, and that I wasn't stopping, affected both my relationship with God and my prayer life-after all, how could you ask for forgiveness when you knew full well that you were planning to do the same sin in just a few hours?

Another area of concern in my Christian walk was the fact that every Christian I respected was against abortion, yet I was not. I figured that it was probably wrong since everyone was so against it. However, no one could ever point to any conclusive evidence in the Bible that God was against it. My walk with God was being stunted because of this issue, but I didn't know how to settle it.

And then I fell. After treating females with respect for 15 months, I met this gorgeous young woman who made it very clear that she would appreciate some disrespectful behavior. I decided to forget about being respectful. She lived in another state, so we corresponded for a while. I ended up leaving my job and moving to be with her. Luckily, our relationship only lasted two months.

God, however, can use any situation to His glory. I moved to Boise, Idaho, and got plugged into another Bible Church. Actually, it wasn't just "another Bible Church." My respect and admiration for the quality of messages that I heard at my church in the other town prompted me to call the seminary that the pastor had attended and inquire if there were any alumni in Boise who were graduates of the same seminary. There were two, and I made my new church home with one of them.

Since attending this church, I'm finally 'on track.' With God's help I have stopped the premeditated sins that I was committing. Furthermore, with His help, I've been able to significantly reduce the number of spontaneous sins that I commit. One of the pastors at this church helped me to search for an answer to my abortion question, and I'm happy to be able to say that now I see that God is against abortion. I have also made fairly significant progress towards cleaning up some of the sins of my past. Of course, I am still tempted regularly. However, I now give the temptations directly to Jesus-as opposed to trying to fight them myself. It's amazing how much easier the battle is once you accept that God really is there fighting for you!

All my life I have been extremely lucky, narrowly escaping death many times, as well as being in the right place at the right time entirely too many times to pin it on coincidence. I have always told people that I had a really big guardian angel. While attending the first Bible Church, I realized that while I hadn't lived the life of a Christian, I had been a Christian since I was 9 years old. What I had thought was a guardian angel was no less than Jesus Christ! The reason I had been so excessively lucky was that I had been 'in' Christ the whole time.

When I finally decided to turn (my life) around and go looking for Jesus-I found Him right behind me. Not only did I not have to go looking for Him, but He actually wanted me just the way I was-with a sinful past; present problems; residual questions, apprehensions, doubts, hesitancies, et cetera! I had been the prodigal son, and yet He had been with me through the entire journey, keeping me safe until I decided on my own to come home. Since all Christians don't experience this kind of "luck," it makes me wonder what His plans are for my life.

Chapter Thirty-seven

Concluding Thoughts

The reason that I went over the last four chapters is because the eternal salvation of your soul is at stake. However, to relate it to your job search, the reason that I shared it was to show you how to be accepted into God's family.

As a non-believer you can pray (for assistance in your job search, for example), but God may not choose to listen. It's kind of like a neighbor kid ringing your doorbell and asking to share his problems with you. You could choose to listen, but you could choose not to also.

However, if your own kid came to you and needed to share some problems, you would be much more inclined to listen. Why? Because you love him, and he is your child. While the dynamics are somewhat different with God (for example, He really does love you, whether you choose to accept His free gift or not), the family analogy remains. He has promised to take care of His children. He has not promised to take care of those who are not his children.

If you feel that God has to listen to you no matter what, consider *Jeremiah 2:27* where it says, "They have turned their backs to Me and not their faces; yet when they are in trouble, they say, 'come and save us!'"...followed by 11:14b where it says, "I WILL NOT LISTEN when they call to Me in the time of their distress." (Emphasis added) Another verse to consider is *Isaiah 59:2,* where it says, "Your iniquities have separated you from your God; your sins have hidden His face from you, so that HE WILL NOT HEAR." (Emphasis added)

In *I Peter 3:12* it says, "For the eyes of the Lord are on the righteous and His ears are attentive to their prayers, but the face of the Lord is against those who do evil." Analyzing this verse, it is easy to see that while His "ears are attentive" to the first group, "the righteous," they are not listening to the second group.

Of course, when we talk about a relationship with God, we're not talking about being "churchy" or "religious." If you define "religion" as all the stuff that man has put between himself and God, such as denominational biases, traditions, ceremonies, and policies that are not truly based upon scripture, God dislikes religion more than anyone!

For example, consider this verse: "They do not cry out to me from their hearts but wail upon their beds. They gather together for grain and new wine but turn away from Me." *Hosea 7:14.* In this verse, the gathering "together for grain and new wine" refers to "religious activities," yet you'll notice that in the very same sentence, these "religious" people are said to "turn away" from God. The point is that He isn't interested so much in whether you go to church. He's interested in whether the "real you" is turning to Him.

You might feel that you are "basically a good person" and that that will earn you an audience with the Lord or the "right" to go to Heaven. If this describes you, please consider *Isaiah 57:12,* where it says, "I will expose YOUR RIGHTEOUSNESS and your works, and they WILL NOT BENEFIT YOU." (Emphasis added) He isn't nearly as interested in what you do externally as He is in what you do internally concerning His Son.

The main reason that I have gone to such pains to cover all of this is because after reading how God has helped me in my various job searches, I wouldn't want you to develop a "prosperity theology." This is a theology in which you believe that God rewards godliness with material blessings, such as a great, new, high-paying job.

According to *I Timothy 6:5,* such a theology is not scriptural. In fact, the Apostle Paul describes those who teach that as being "destitute of the truth." The main reason for this is that it encourages perverted motives. God wants us to seek Him for His own sake, not for a payoff of physical well-being or financial gain. The reward of loving obedience is a closer relationship to God *(John 14:15-18, 21-23).* He also wants us to be content with what He provides us, not greedy for more *(I Timothy 6:6).*

If you're one of the many people whose main gripe about church has to do with all the hypocrisy that goes on, let me share a thought with you on this. People are not perfect; therefore, no organization made up of people can be perfect. In fact, if you ever do find a "perfect" church, please don't join–being imperfect yourself, you'll ruin it!

The thing to keep in mind is that the main reason for going to church should be to worship God, and develop your relationship with Him. It's certainly scriptural to build relationships with the pastor and other members of the congregation; however, you should know that they will let you down. After all, they are only human! Consider the following.

> Have you quit eating just because Mom once burned the biscuits? They didn't look good or taste good and had lost most of their food value. "Well," you say, "I need to eat and besides, Mom didn't mean to burn the biscuits."

> Have you quit going to the doctor because you once read about a doctor practicing without a license? "Of course not," you reply. "Some 'quack' isn't going to keep me from going to a good doctor."

> Have you thrown away all your money because someone once passed you a counterfeit dollar? The answer is obvious.

So now let's apply the same common sense to the spiritual dimension of your life. It is quite possible that someone may have offended you as he tried to explain being "born again" or "being saved." Perhaps his way of doing it left a bad taste in your mouth.

You may have been wronged but you can't just say, "I don't want anything more to do with becoming a Christian." You have spiritual needs that are as real as the body's need for food. And the fact remains—you still need the forgiveness of sins.

Every occupation has people who will use illegal or harmful practices for their own advantage. Isn't it logical that some of these same people will try to operate under the guise of Christianity? The very fact that Christians usually do not act in a deceitful way makes it that much easier for spiritual quacks to fool people. So to classify all Christians as quacks would be a big mistake.

As long as there is a real thing there will always be an imitation. You will never see a counterfeit three-dollar bill because there isn't a real three-dollar bill. Since there is reality to Christian faith there will always be hypocrites or counterfeit Christians.

Each person needs to have a right relationship to God. Forget how man has confused or misrepresented the message or how your own heart has tried to explain things away.

It may be all too true that you have seen spiritual counterfeits or quacks. You may have known some Christians who were offensive. Still, the decision to believe in the truth of Jesus Christ is yours to make, regardless of how others may have mishandled it. Don't let "burned biscuits" keep you from getting right with God!

He is real. He loves you. He wants you. And He's promised to help you IF you are one of His. If you are not yet one of His, please consider Part III of this book very carefully. If you are one of His, then be sure to include Him in your job search as the vital part of it that He is. My greatest times of spiritual growth have been when I was between jobs and *had* to rely on Him. This can also be a time of incredible spiritual growth for you, if you let it be. It's up to you.

To conclude this part of the book, let me share two little bumper sticker-type quotes. The first one may be new to you, the other one's a repeat from a few pages ago. Here they are: "There are only two kinds of people–those who have met Him, and those who will." And, "What you do with Him will determine what He'll do with you." Think about it!

In conclusion, thank you for allowing me to share my advice with you. I would also like to wish you the very best as you begin, or continue, your job search.

Appendices

Appendix I

Sample Reference-Check Form

Name of Employment Applicant: _____

- What were the dates of employment?
- What positions did he/she hold?
- What was his/her final salary?
- In the position, what were his/her duties?
- How would you describe his/her work?
- How did he/she get along with co-workers?
- What are his/her strong points?
- How would you describe his/her attendance?
- How much, and what kind of, supervision did he/she require?
- What reservations should I have about hiring him/her?
- Who else could comment on his/her performance?
- Why did he/she leave your employ?
- Would you rehire him/her?
- Are there any final comments that you would like to make?

Name of Reference: _____

Employer and Title: _____

Date of Reference: _____

Relationship to Employment Applicant: _____

Appendix II

101 Sample Interview Questions

- Tell me about yourself.
- What do you really want to do in life?
- How would you describe yourself?
- What leadership roles have you held?
- Give some examples that support your interest in _____.
- What did you gain from your past job experiences?
- Why did you choose your particular field of work?
- Which is more important to you, money or the type of job?
- How would a good friend or former supervisor describe you?
- What motivates you to put forth your greatest effort?
- How do you determine or evaluate success?
- What qualities should a successful manager possess?
- What type of relationship should exist between supervisors and employees?
- What accomplishments have given you the most satisfaction? Why?
- In what kind of work environment are you most comfortable?
- How do you work under pressure?
- How do you deal with frustration? Stress? Anxiety? Pressures?
- How would you describe the ideal job?
- What two or three things are most important to you in your job?
- What criteria are you using to evaluate the company for which you hope to work?
- What was the first job you ever had?

- Do you feel that you have received a good general training?
- Do you like routine work?
- How do you feel about overtime?
- Can you get recommendations from previous employers?
- Are you looking for a part-time, a temporary, or a "permanent" job?
- What are your special abilities?
- Are you seeking employment in a company of a certain size? Why?
- If you were starting all over again, what field would you choose? Why?
- Are you an honest/ambitious/creative/etc. person? Can you give examples?
- What does "customer service" mean to you?
- Are you more of a "people person," or are you more "task-oriented"?
- If you had to summarize your entire being into one word or phrase, what would that one word or phrase be?
- Are you willing to spend at least six months as a trainee?
- Can you think of any questions that I should ask you that I haven't?
- What are your long-range and short-range goals and objectives, when and why did you establish these goals, and how are you preparing yourself to achieve them?
- What specific goals, other than those related to your occupation, have you established for yourself for the next 10 years?
- What do you really want to do in life?
- What are the most important rewards you expect in your business career?
- What do you see yourself doing five years from now?
- What do you expect to be earning in five years?
- In school, what courses did you like the best? Least? Why?
- What was your GPA (and if it was low, why was it so low)?

- Describe your most rewarding college experience
- If you could do so, how would you plan your academic study differently?
- Do you have plans for continued study? An advanced degree?
- Do you feel your grades are a good indication of your academic success?
- Tell me about your extracurricular activities and interests.
- What have you learned from participation in extracurricular activities?
- What extracurricular offices have you held?
- What percentage of your college expenses did you earn? How?
- How did you spend your vacations while in school?
- Why did you select your college or university?
- What led you to choose your field of major study?
- Would you prefer on-the-job training or formal programs?
- In what jobs have you been most interested?
- What jobs have you held? How were they obtained and why did you leave?
- What is your experience in supervision?
- Tell me about a team you've been on and what your role in it was,
- What major problems have you encountered and how did you deal with them?
- What have you learned from your mistakes?
- Tell me of a disagreement you had with a co-worker and how it was resolved.
- Tell me of a disagreement you had with a supervisor and how it was resolved.
- Why would you be successful in this position?
- How has your background prepared you for this position?

- Why should I hire you?
- Why should we hire you for this job rather than anyone else?
- What do you think it takes to be successful in this company?
- How can you make a contribution to our company?
- If you were hiring for this position, what qualities would you look for?
- Why do you think you might like to work for our company?
- What do you know about this company?
- What are your salary expectations?
- Why do you think you would like this job?
- What would you do if...? (Imagine situations that test your knowledge of the job)
- What interests you about our product or service?
- What is your strongest qualification for this position?
- How do you think you will fit into our operations?
- Would you like to live in the community where our company is located? Why?
- Will you relocate? Does relocating bother you?
- Do you have a geographical preference?
- Are you willing to travel?
- How do you spend your spare time?
- What are your strongest personal qualities?
- What are your weakest personal qualities?
- What special or unique qualifications do you have that make you feel that you will be successful in this field? In this company? In this position?
- What is the last book you read?
- As a child, who was your hero? Who are your current heroes?
- Have you ever had your driver's license revoked?

- How long do you expect to work?
- Have you ever been fired from a job?
- Why have you been unemployed for all this time?
- Why did you contact me?
- What do you like best/least about the type of work you do?
- Have you ever thought about going into business for yourself?
- Why do you want to change fields now?
- Well, Mr./Mrs. _____, what can I do for you?
- Why have you held so many jobs?
- Why do you want to leave your present position?
- Does your employer know you are planning to leave?
- Is there anything else that you'd like to share about yourself?

Appendix III

Miscellaneous Job Search Guidelines

- Be honest and truthful, conduct your job search with integrity.
- Be yourself–but the best *you* possible.
- It's generally easier to get a job when you have a job.
- Attitude can be everything.
- Your resume won't get you a job; its job is to get you an interview.
- Apply for a specific position.
- Lack of qualifications is not as negative as a bad presentation of yourself.
- Timing is a critical factor. Being in the right place at the right time or applying when there's an opening is key.
- Blindly mailing resumes (with or without cover letters) to companies that are not advertising positions is a waste of time and money. Most companies file them away and never refer to them again.
- There's a thin line between enthusiasm and being overbearing. Find out from your contact (the person to whom you are applying) when and how often you should check back.
- Smile, and be friendly and polite to everyone with whom you come in contact. Frequently, well-qualified people don't get the job because of the way they treated the receptionist.
- Do not mention any affiliation with special interest, political, or religious groups unless you are applying for a job with an organization that fully supports the work of those groups.

- Be as certain as you can be that you like, and can do, the work you are applying for.
- Be able to give a continuous record of all your jobs, dates of employment, wages received, supervisors, employer addresses and phone numbers, your duties and responsibilities, your job titles, and the reasons for leaving.

Would You Like Some Professional Help With

Your Job Search?

The Job Search Advisor, Incorporated, is available to personally assist you with your job search. Services include:

- **Individualized consultations**–most clients only need 2-3 hours. With a minimum 2-hour consultation, you also get free telephone follow-up. This is an excellent opportunity to find out what you're doing wrong, and how to fix it. Techniques and strategies relevant to *your* job search will be covered. Possible topics include interviewing and networking skills, using the Internet, salary negotiation, handling tough interview questions, resume review, job search research, dealing with prejudice, and information on area associations. Customized Job Search Plan of Action developed upon request.

- **Mock interview followed by professional critique**–Ideal for job seekers who get interviews but no job offers. One of our experienced hiring authorities will conduct an interview and then offer you specific advice on how to improve your future interviews.

- **Career counseling**–If you're not sure of what you want to do with the rest of your professional career, The Job Search Advisor can help! We offer a career assessment, followed by a career consultation.

- **Reference check service**–An opportunity to find out what your previous employers are *really* saying about you.

- **The Job Search Advisor will help you get hired sooner, for more pay, and into a job you'll enjoy.**

To find a location near you, or for a telephone consultation, contact The Job Search Advisor today!

www.jobsearchadvisor.com

(208) 463-2375

Note to experienced hiring authorities:
Job Search Advisor Business Opportunities are now available!
Please check out our website, and then contact us if qualified and interested.

About the Author

Mr. Gilliam's professional experience includes being staffing manager, recruiter, senior career transition specialist, job search consultant, personnel coordinator, and senior human resource specialist for public, private, and non-profit employers. He has developed and presented job search seminars for the United States military, State Departments, universities, and corporations. His experience encompasses most every industry and field imaginable.

He is the founder of The Job Search Advisor, Incorporated, a consulting firm that he started in 1995. He has published more than 50 articles on how to conduct a successful job search and is regularly featured on *Career Clinic*, a nationally syndicated radio program aired on more than 40 radio stations across North America as well as the military's international radio network.

As a recruiter, he has reviewed thousands of resumes and has interviewed hundreds of people. His recruiting experience encompasses all levels of employees. This includes high-level executives, managers, engineers, airline pilots, and doctors, as well as seasonal, temporary, and part-time positions-and, of course, every level of position in between.

As a career counselor, he has spent countless hours doing one-on-one sessions with employees, helping them decide the best direction for their careers, reviewing and revising their resumes, conducting mock interviews and then critiquing them, discussing individual networking strategies, and helping people deal with prejudices in their job searches.

Mr. Gilliam's academic credentials include a bachelor's degree in administrative management, several graduate-level courses related to human resources, and more than two dozen professional seminars. Furthermore, prior to earning the Senior Professional in Human Resources (SPHR) designation in 1999 through the Society for Human Resource Management's Human Resource Certification Institute, he was a twice-certified Professional in Human Resources (PHR).

As far as practicing what he preaches, Mr. Gilliam has been on the other side of the desk several times. Due to layoffs and to further his career, he has conducted many job searches himself. This has allowed him the opportunity to use the advice he gives others.

Mr. Gilliam was born and reared in Alaska. He was a military brat as a child and then attended junior high and high school in his hometown of Homer, Alaska. He was an entrepreneur and adventurer during college and throughout his 20s. As an adult, he has worked in many states. He is currently expanding his consulting business, The Job Search Advisor, Incorporated, nationwide; as well as continuing to be a practicing H.R. professional, author, lecturer, and job search consultant (Career Transition Specialist).

He and his wife, Christy, have two little girls, Nakeata and Syaira. Pets include a horse, two big outdoor dogs, and several fish. Both he and his wife have accepted the Lord Jesus Christ as their personal Savior.